Wicca Book for Beginners

Learn Wicca, Witchcraft, Beliefs, Ritual Magic, Spells, Coven, Divination, Traditional and Contemporary Paths

Frank Bawdoe

Copyright 2021 - All rights reserved.

It is not legal to reproduce, duplicate, or transmit any part of this document in either electronic means or in printed format. Recording of this publication is strictly prohibited and any storage of this document is not allowed unless with written permission from the publisher except for the use of brief quotations in a book review.

Disclaimer: Any medicinal benefits given here are a product of my own research and as such should not be taken over the advice of trained medical professionals. Always make sure that anything you consume is 100% safe. If you are pregnant, consult your doctor or midwife before consuming something you haven't tried before

SPECIAL BONUS!

Thank you for adding this book to your Wiccan Library! To learn more, why not join Frank's Wiccan Community and get this additional Free Wicca Starter Kit Book 100% FREE!

Hundreds of others are already enjoying insider access to all of my current and future full-length books, 100% free!

If you want insider access plus this Free Wicca Starter Kit Book, all you have to do is **scan the code below** with your smartphone camera to claim your offer!

Table of Contents

Wicca for Beginners 1

Introduction 3
1. What is Wicca? 6
2. The Core Beliefs & The Deities of Wicca 23
3. The Wiccan Holidays & Festivals of The
   Wheels of The Year 32
4. The Overview of Wiccan Covens, Circles,
   Solitary Practice & the Magic of The Witch 51
5. Initiation Techniques, Forms of Wicca &
   Types of Witches 89

Afterword 101
Sources 102

Modern Witchcraft for Beginners 105

Introduction 107
1. What is Witchcraft? 110

2. How to Learn Magic in the Modern World.....155

3. Different Types of Witchcraft and Witches 179

4. Witchcraft Supplies and the Witch's Common Tools 203

5. Herbal Magic for Witches...................................224

6. Step by Step Guide to Rituals and Crafting Spells..251

Final Thoughts 263

Sources..266

Wicca for Beginners

Learn Wicca, Magic, Rituals, Witchcraft & Beliefs with This Easy to Read Guide

Introduction

Wicca is a pagan religion based on nature and practiced with a strict ethical code. It is a modern-day doctrine that honors both a female goddess and a male god, incorporates natural objects and herbalism, and includes the celebration of equinoxes and solstices. Practiced by individuals or covens (group members), Wiccans claim a direct connection to ancient pre-Christian traditions. There is no single Wiccan authority as some are solo witches and some worship in covens. Wicca is someone who believes in the wiccan religion who has knowledge of Pagans and follows their paths provided by Wicca. This book will teach beginners about the history, principles, ethics, philosophy, rituals, and witchcraft of Wicca. Witches maintain the belief that the mind of a human has the power to create change with methods not yet comprehended by science. As part of their ceremonial rituals, spells of healing are performed, as well as honoring their deities. Their code of ethics prohibits any magic harmful to anyone and is only helpful. As a matter of fact, the Wicca religion asserts that negative magic comes back magnified on the perpetrator. Frank Bawdoe introduces Wicca as a present-day gentle and nature-oriented religion committed to God and Goddess and addresses the most important issues of today.

Frank Bawdoe is a devotee of spiritualism and an author who shares a deep-rooted fascination with the philosophy of Wicca and Paganism. Driven by the desire to help the masses embrace spirituality, he aspires to ignite the flames of appreciation in the hearts and minds of readers who are passionate about exploring the essence of life. To explore the realm of paganism and comprehend the depths of Wicca, Frank devotes his time to understanding the principles, philosophies, rituals, and beliefs that define this exceptional modern pagan religion.

Frank Bawdoe has authored numerous books on Wicca and Paganism, including Witchcraft Religion & Spirituality and New Age Divination. An ardent knowledge seeker who proudly walks the path leading to spirituality, he leverages his knowledge to understand the fascinating ways of life. Exploring the depths of paganism with utmost faith and persistence for truth, Frank studies the Wiccan culture, meditation, visualization, magic, and spells to build a better connection with his inner self. Passionate about transforming lives and directing souls, Frank Bawdoe pens down his knowledge to help others get one step closer to spirituality. With his words, he shines a light on the path leading to self- development, happiness, and spirituality. Frank never ceases to miss out on an opportunity to embrace the beauty of life and surrounds himself with nature that scintillates the soul and soothes the mind. He devotes his free time to read, write, meditate, and explore the mysteries of life.

Chapter One:

WHAT IS WICCA?

WICCA IS A RELIGION DEDICATED TO THE BETTERMENT OF MANKIND AND WOMANKIND.

The word Wicca stems from the word wicce (Anglo-Saxon) meaning to shape or bend nature to your assistance. Based on beliefs in existence long before Christ, Wicca ascertains that Magic is real and exists on the Earth. It pays tribute to the elements and nature and worships two deities, the Moon Goddess and the Horned God. The Moon Goddess and the Horned God represent the feminine and masculine energies of the universe and of nature. It differs from Paganism in that there is more freedom of religion. The God and Goddess simply exist as opposing forces of creation. However, a witch must devote themselves to the Wiccan Rede, "As it harms none, do as thou wilt."

HISTORY OF WICCA

Wicca started in the early twentieth century, developed in England among covens who based their religious practices on the works of writers such as Margaret Murry and other historical Witch-groups. A British born occultist by the name of Gerald Gardner is one of the first and most famous Wiccans. Born in 1884, Gardner was a member of a group of Witches known as the New Forest Coven. Gardner followed the teachings of another Witch by the name of Aleister Crowely and he then went on to be the founder of the modern-day Wicca religion. By the 1950s Gardner's practice spread into Australia, Great Britain, and the United States.

It was Gardner's development of the Wiccan religion that started changing people's perceptions regarding Witchcraft into a more positive direction. Prior to Gardner, Witchcraft was often seen as satanic and barbarous. He also came about in a time where men could be known as Witches. Before this, Witches were usually accused of blasphemy and were almost always female. If a woman stood out for being independent, intelligent, or sexual in nature they were accused of being devil- worshipers because they dared to venture outside of society's expectations of women at the time. The only time men were ever accused of being a Witch is when they were flamboyant or homosexual.

Gardner became familiar with magical practices and occult concepts while he was working in Asia. He studied the work of British occultist Aleister Crowley and other Western literature ideologies of esotericism. Just before the start of World War II, Gardner returned to England and became involved in the British occult community and became the founder of the modern-day Wiccan religion.

Covens usually have approximately 10 members and through a ritual they are initiated. As the members of the coven master their magic practices and learn the Wiccan rituals, they go through up to three degrees. The third degree is for those who want to enter into the priesthood. Following Gardner's system, priestesses are giving priority.

Paganism today refers to those who follow a spiritual journey through life that is rooted in nature, seasonal cycles, and astronomical patterns. Some identify themselves as polytheists in that they honor more than a single god. Wicca is one of the many ethereal paths that fall under the description of Paganism. Asatruar, Druids, Celtic Pagans, and reconstructionists are some of the other types of Paganism. Each branch has its own specific set of traditions, beliefs, and practices. Each branch of Paganism can practice in different ways from each other because there is no universal set of rules or guidelines.

The practice of Magic may have been around since the beginning of civilization, but it has blossomed over the millennia. As the word spread since 1950, the definition of a Wicca has developed into a positive religious practice. It is imperative that even people who are not Witches or practice magic understand what is entailed in being a Witch. It is important to note that the magic practiced by Witches is very natural and not the sensationalized mystery the press often plays up. With the appropriate education, Wicca will become as normalized in society as other accepted religions.

PRINCIPLES OF WICCA

It is customary in most Wiccan covens to have some type of initiation to symbolically represent rebirth, where the newly initiated dedicate themselves to the goddess and god of their choosing. A High Priestess or High Priest of the Third-Degree rank conducts the initiation. It is usually a year and a day of study to advance to the next degree. However, if not a coven member, an individual can choose to a ritual to self-dedicate himself or herself to the Gods of their journey. All followers of the Wicca religion believe in the use of spells and magic, not as a supernatural entity, but as the redirection and harnessing of natural energy to create change. Magic is used as a tool or a skill and can be used by anyone with a bit of practice. Spell crafting tools most commonly used are herbs, candles, athame, crystals, wands, and other special items. Often the magical workings of Witches are performed in a sacred circle with a set of ethical guidelines on why and how the magic should be enacted.

Found in most Wiccan practices are the following core tenets:

- The Divine exists in nature and therefore, nature should be respected and honored. Everything from trees and plants, to animals and rocks are sacred elements. Within the Divine is a goddess and a god to be honored. Since we are all sacred the Divine is present in each one of us, making us all sacred beings worthy of interacting with the god and goddess. Interacting with a Divine entity is not limited just to a select coven or to the priesthood.
- Afterlife and Karma is viewed as a sort of cosmic payback system in that what a person does in their lifetime will be reencountered upon in the next. There is not a belief in the concepts of hell, sin, or heaven.

- Ancestors are to be honored in the Wiccan religion as it is not unusual for Witches to communicate with the spirit world. Many Witches believe their ancestors are by their side at all times.
- Wiccan holidays are centered around the cycle of seasons and the turning of the earth. There are eight days of power (Sabbats) celebrated along with Esbats on a monthly basis.
- In Wiccan tradition each person is responsible for their own actions. Personal responsibility is a central aspect of the Wicca religion and each member must be willing to accept the good or bad consequences of their behavior.
- Harm no one is a common concept of the Wiccan tradition and means there should be no intentional harm done to another being.
- Non-judgmentalism and without coercion, is the common practice of the Wiccans. Covenants and individual practitioners must find their own spiritual journey and respect the beliefs of others in the process.

TRADITIONS OF WICCA

Wiccans generally accept the concept of an afterlife, and there is a general acceptance of interactions with the spirit world. While not all Witches seek to interact with the dead, many do practice séances and contact with the unknown. Astrology, runes, and tarot divinations are commonly used as methods of communication with other worldly entities.

RULE OF THREE

Some Witches follow the "Rule of Three' also known as the Law of Threefold Return, while others may adhere to the Wiccan Rede. The Law of Threefold Return or the Rule of was designed to encourage a new Witch to think of the consequences of performing any negative magic. Many new Witches are initiated with words of caution from their elders that if they do not honor the Rule of Three when practicing their magic, bad deeds will be revisited upon them three-fold. Some debate the pagan theory of the Rule of Three as a scare tactic to influence new Witches, others say it is only a guideline to keep Witches compliant with the Wiccan code of ethics, and still other covenants swear by it.

It can be an unsettling thought that Witches are going around tossing hexes and curses at people and situations, so the Law of Threefold Return is an effective means for inspiring thought before action.

While this law sounds prohibitive, most Wiccans use it as a standard to live by. One may ask, "Why is it called the Rule of *Three*?" It is because three is accepted as a magical number. Pythagoras, the ancient Greek philosopher theorized that the meaning of numbers was very significant. In his eyes the number 3 was thought of as the perfect number signifying the beginning, middle, and end; birth, life, and death; past, present, and future; wisdom, harmony, and understanding; the divine number. It can mean literally three times, or it can mean three times worse. It could also mean that negative actions affect you on three levels: spiritual, emotional, and physical. Another interpretation of those who believe in reincarnation is that the Rule of Three is a cosmic one: what you do in this life will affect you threefold in the next life. Likewise, your life today is a reflection of what you have done in past lives whether they are good deeds or bad. Ultimately, whether you decide to believe in the Law of Threefold Return as a segment in life's little book of instructions, it is up to you to take responsibility for your own behavior and your magic.

TYPES OF WITCHCRAFT

Gardnerian

The Gardnerian tradition appropriately named after Gerald Gardner follows the core ethical guideline of

The Wiccan Rede: to do as you like but harm no one. The word rede refers to giving counsel or advice. It is not a rule but a guideline. Gardnerian witches are firmly against any type of coercion and believe in an informed consent. As aforementioned in the Law of Three, thinking before action is a clear expression of free will. This philosophy implies that whatever intentions are placed into this world will be returned thrice multiplied. This concept strongly supports the importance of causing no harm. Gardnerian Wiccans follow these tradition-based instructions that demand thought especially before spell work. Gardnerian Wicca differs from other modern witchcraft practices that focus on the sole practitioner's spiritual development.

Gardnerian Wicca is a non-dogmatic religion that allows each initiate to find their own meaning or ritualistic experiences by the use of shared ritual traditions. The focus is on correct practice (orthopraxy) not on correct thinking (orthodoxy) and therefore emphasizes shared practices rather than shared faith.

Alexandrian

Influenced by Gardnerian philosophy, Alex and Maxine Sanders branched off from the Gardnerian coven to start Alexandrian Wicca in the 1960s. The main focus in Alexandrian Wicca are the ceremonies and rites dedicating equal time to the Goddess and God; gender polarity. Alexandrian Wiccans gather in covens during the eight Wiccan Sabbats, full moons, and new moons, and work with ceremonial magic.

Alexandrians emphasize the importance of the wiccan rite of passage, or initiation. Prior to initiation, coven members decide if the person will be a good fit with their coven by interviewing the initiate and through invitations to gatherings and open rituals. An offer to join officially is made and if accepted, the new initiate starts to study without being bound to the vows of the coven. This first phase can last up to a year depending on the member. The potential member is exposed to the close coven bond as well as the elders being exposed to the candidate. Traditionally, the decision is matrifocal, meaning the final decision is made by the high priestess. If welcomed into the coven, the candidate will then have the choice to achieve the first degree of initiation and commit himself or herself to a more serious path. Here the new member must show dedication to the learning and commitment to the craft's knowledge and show great enthusiasm toward learning the ways of the craft. Alexandrian Wiccan tradition believes that all members are priestesses and priests, meaning that every coven member has the ability to participate in a fellowship with the Divine, therefore there are no "lay persons".

Eclectic

Eclectic Wicca is a term given to witchcraft traditions that do not fit into any specified category. It is common for Solitaries to follow an eclectic path, but there are also eclectic covens. An eclectic approach to Wicca utilizes a combination of practices and beliefs from various different traditions and pantheons. Some covens may modify Gardnerian or Alexandrian methods making them different. If a belief or practice cannot be defined, it is termed eclectic. A solo practitioner who is uninitiated may be exercising the craft they have learned from available resources regarding Wicca, but not be bound to the initiation process, and therefore, acknowledges their practice is eclectic. There is some debate as to whether non-lineage covens should be able to refer to themselves as Wiccans, but can be acknowledged as NeoWicca, or non- traditional, new Wiccan. As is customary with all Wiccan traditions there are no insulting or derogatory aspects.

Traditional

Traditional Wicca is usually termed so mainly in the U.S. and applies to groups following Wiccan traditions that originated in England's New Forest region. Traditional Wiccans strictly adhere to Gardner's initiatory lineage and not to NeoWiccanism or eclectic traditions. Traditional Wiccan initiates work with deities who are secret in name as to preserve their sacredness. Traditional Wiccan follows a coven-based practice. Even if there is not a traditional Wiccan coven near your area, you can still find traditional Wiccans who may be willing to share their knowledge and mentor new initiates. As witchcraft continues to evolve with each new generation of witches, varying types of witchcraft will change with the times and with the communities and cultures that practice them. However, traditional Wicca has thrived and survived through changing times and will undoubtedly carry on, even though many don't even realize it is there.

Hereditary

There is no one person biologically born Wiccan, just as there is no one born Muslim, Hindu, or Christian. The Wiccan religion is not orthopraxic, meaning that you believe or act in certain ways that makes you Wiccan. You can indeed be raised by Wiccans, but that does not mean you inherited Wiccan DNA. There are those who have been encouraged to tap into their psychic abilities while growing up, but that does not make them any different biologically or chromosomally. People can inherit family and cultural traditions making them more prone to discover their own spiritual journey in the Wiccan religion. Some claim a hereditary Witch comes from a family that has practiced Witchcraft for hundreds of years and have had the Old Religion passed down over many generations. It is important to note that even when referred to as a hereditary Witch, it may only mean they are third or fourth generation Wiccans.

COMMON MYTHS AND MISCONCEPTIONS

In 1986 Wicca was recognized by the Court of Appeals as a legitimate religion. However, Wiccans are still a generally misunderstood group. Many Witches prefer to be titled Wiccans because of the severe negative connotations associated with the practice of Witchcraft. One very false and negative belief is that Wiccans cast harmful spells. Actually, as aforementioned, it is very much against the Wiccan creed to harm another. Based loosely on paganism's rituals and rites centuries ago, the reverence for the celebrations related to magic, seasons, and the harvest remain the center point of the Wiccan religion. The United States government has deemed Wicca as an official religion, with holidays, varying by state, observed. For instance, eight Wiccan holidays are observed by the New Jersey Department of Education, including Mabon (the beginning of autumn), and allows Wiccan children to be excused from school on those days. Wiccans are entitled to the same rights as any other individual's rights in taking their spiritual path in life.

Another commonly held misconception is that Wiccans are Satan worshipers, when in fact, Wiccans do not even believe in the devil at all. The concepts of heaven and hell have never been a part of the Wiccan religion. They do not believe in only one God, but in goddesses and gods, similar to Hinduism and Buddhism. Likewise, the sacrifice of animals is a misconception of the Wiccan religion. The Wiccan religion is based on nature and Witches have respect for all things living. They may offer a sacrifice to their deities, but they are usually in the form of flowers, bread, wine, or fruit. Wiccans are animal lovers and have a law against any type of blood sacrifice.

There is no Holy Bible that Wiccans follow. They may create a "Book of Shadows (BoS)," or have one passed down from a teacher or family member, but the BoS is only used as a book of reference. Witches also commonly keep a magical diary (grimoire), in which Wiccans keep a record of useful information for practicing their craft, ceremonies, rituals, and spells. Wiccans do cast spells, and the practice of magic is thought to be completely natural. Wiccans believe magic is part of nature and to be used for a variety of good such as healing, prosperity, and personal growth.

Even though Wiccans can be considered somewhat sexually liberal and completely non-judgmental, does that mean they are frequently involved in orgies? Nope! They really do not get involved in the gossip of who is sleeping with who. As long as the adults are consenting, Wiccans do not care if you're gay, straight, transgendered, bisexual, or anything else. Likewise, Witches are not all women. The origin of the Witches legacy is undeniably gendered female but that is because it is a history perpetuated by sexism and misogyny that in the first place demonized Witchcraft and Witches. Witches come in all forms, shapes, and sizes, male, female, transgendered, and of all ethnic origins. Throughout history Witches were persecuted females, while men who practiced magic were revered as sorcerers and magicians. Witches were considered a threat because they did not conform to gender and societal norms which was dangerous in the eyes of a patriarchal hierarchy society.

Contrary to some beliefs, you are not born a Witch. There is always some problematic person insisting they were born a Witch because they come from a magical bloodline. While magical ancestors are a powerful influence, they have nothing to do with whether or not you can be a Witch. Some things are very real in the world of Witchcraft, hexes are real, which is why in part for the Rule of Three, but this rule also applies to positive magic. When it comes to hexes, a commonly used term is black magic. First of all, this can be misconstrued to have racist undertones, while white magic is considered good. Magic is neither evil or good; it is a tool and an avenue for spiritual expression.

You need not have to have years and years of training from confirmed witches before you can cast your first spell and it does not require a full moon, coven, or animal bones to enact them. Casting a spell simply means putting an intention forth and then conducting a ritual to fulfill it, be that mediating, praying, or lighting a candle. For example, let's say each morning you want to awaken with loads of self-confidence. Write an affirmation letter telling yourself how special you are and that you honor the Goddess of beauty and love, Venus, or a deity you feel personally connected to. Simply making a gratitude list and repeating a chant is harnessing that energy and casting a spell.

Witchery is not an expensive practice. With its rise in popularity, witchcraft is now more accessible and the myth that it is evil is becoming debunked. However, here is a heads-up on the Witchcraft industry, many scammers are out there trying to cash in. It isn't necessary to spend a hundred bucks on goop or bags of crystals. Incense, rituals, tarot cards, and candles can help refine your practice. But all that is really needed to practice magic is you. You are more powerful than any items you can buy.

You do not need to be a member of a coven to be a Witch and there are also less governed groups of Witches who practice together in a more casual manner than those covens with highly organized processes of initiation. Others still prefer to be solo Witches. Each person's spiritual journey is very personal, so whether or not to be a member of a coven is up to you.

Chapter Two:

THE CORE BELIEFS & THE DEITIES OF WICCA

WICCANS TODAY HAVE USED THEIR INNOVATIONS TO TRANSFORM ANCIENT PRACTICES of Witchcraft to meet the needs of modern-day spirituality. However, older traditions still offer problems to society and governments worldwide. Educators and scholars of traditional Wiccan still teach the psychosocial realities of witchcraft and the still present dangers of persecution. Contemporary Wicca draws in people who tend to have an empowering nature, giving individuals the ability to shape their own future and giving a voice to those who have commonly been silenced.

While Wicca has much in common with Paganism, modern Wiccan covens celebrate diversity and do not have a single bound set of practices, beliefs, or texts. Some are sticklers for prehistoric philosophies, or they try to revive ancient and indigenous practices as accurately as possible. Wiccans focus on an improved future and see all religions as equal, whereas traditional Paganism accounts for the differences between polytheistic and monotheistic religious practices.

GODS AND GODDESSES

Two major deities are worshiped in the Wicca religion: The Triple Goddess and the Great Horned God. Some Wiccans view these deities as male and female aspects of greatness, and some worship them equally along with other special deities from a variety of pantheons. As previously discussed, many Wiccan Gods and Goddesses are connected to the past with emphasis on healing, protection, love, fertility, and the harvest.

THE TRIPLE GODDESS

The aspects of the Triple Goddess can be connected to several ancient civilizations' beliefs, such as Hera, who has the aspects of Woman, Widow, and Girl. Another example is the Celtic goddess Brigid who had the aspects of smithcraft, healing, and poetry. In the Wiccan religion, the Triple Goddess represents the Mother, Maiden, and the Crone. The Triple

Goddess aspects align with the Moon's phases and its cycle of orbits around the earth. These three aspects delineate the cycles in a woman's life of reproducing: premenstrual, childbearing, and menopause. However, a woman literally goes through these cycles in her lifetime, but the aspects also represent male qualities of the human psyche as the circle of life is experienced by all living beings on the Earth.

The Maiden

When the moon is taking its first step toward being full it is known as the crescent-to-waxing phase. When new, the moon is completely invisible until a sliver of illumination appears, this is the aspect of the Maiden's youthfulness. The Maiden is associated with sunrise, dawn, and the season of Spring; it is a time of spiritual growth. The Maiden accents the fresh potential and newness of life. The qualities of independence, innocence, intelligence, and youth are all associated with the Maiden. Witches may refer to the Greek Goddesses Persephone and Artemis, Rhiannon (Celtic), Freya (Nordic), and other deities. The Maiden is also known to be the first in the series of aspects associated with the Triple Goddess. The Maiden is The Virgin and The Huntress and commonly used in rituals and magic associated with all types of new beginnings, such as new homes, new jobs, and new love.

The Mother

The Maiden transforms into the Mother when the Moon turns full, giving the Earth abundance. The Mother represents Summer's midday, with fields and forests flourishing; a lush time of the year bridled with maturing young animals, nurturing, new responsibilities, and adulthood. Considered to be the most powerful of the three aspects of The Goddess, The Mother Goddess aspects was the inspiration for Gerald Gardner's perception of the divine feminine. At many Wiccan altars, the Mother Goddess is represented by the Roman Goddess Ceres, the Greek Goddesses Selene, and Demeter, and Ceres, the Roman Goddess, as well as others.

The Crone

Referred to as the "Hag" in ancient utterances of the Triple Goddess, the Crone takes over power as the darkness grows and the Moon slowly diminishes. The Crone is the post-childbearing aspect and is associated with the night-time and the sunset. The Crone represents Autumn and Winter and the growing season coming to an end. As the older and wiser aspect of the Triple Goddess, the Crone governs endings; aging-death- rebirth, transformations, past lives, prophecy, visions, and guidance. The Crone has been feared for millennia as a reminder that death is part of the circle of life, just like the dark phase of the Moon comes before the New Moon. The Crone has been slandered because of being misunderstood, probably because of the way many in our society view the elderly. In many cultures the elderly is honored for their wisdom, but in some cultures, the elderly is a reminder of death and sometimes pawned off to healthcare workers as a matter of convenience. The Crone is referred to as The Wise One and has great wisdom to impart. The Crone is Winter, death, and represented by the waning moon and the color black.

THE HORNED GOD

The Horned God is said to travel through the forests as a protector of the Goddesses and all of her children. He is referred to by many other entities such as the God of the hunt, forest, and flock. The God of Life and the God of Death and Resurrection; the hunter and the hunted; the darkness and the light. An ancient wall painting of a man dressed in animal skiing adorned with antlers on its head was first created during the Paleolithic period. He is thought to symbolize a sacred dance by the God to magically increase the number of animals for the hunt. Symbols of the Horned God have been noted in Egypt, Babylonia, and Mesopotamia portraying him as the giver of fertility, Death, and Resurrection. The Horned God's symbol is the Sun, as the Moon is the Goddess's symbol. The Horned God oversees the dark half or the Winter months of the year. At some Wiccan celebrations or rituals, the High Priest will act out the image of the Horned God by wearing a Horned Helmet. Some traditional Witchcraft names for the Horned God include Pan of Arcadia, Dionysus of Greece, Herne, England's the Hunter, and the Celtic name, Cernunnos.

Animal fertility has always been important as is human fertility as a means of survival. But the fertility of the crops is also an important aspect of survival, and for these reasons both The Horned God and The Triple Goddess are fertility deities. As the counterpart to the Triple Goddess, the Horned God grants strength, bravery, male virility, and adventure; he is primal and strong. The Horned God can represent three aspects, like the Triple Goddess, that of the Warrior or Youth, the Father, and the Sage. However, sometimes the Triple Goddess aspects and the two Horned God aspects (night and day) are often mapped as five points of the Pentagram.

ANTI-WITCHERY

Whether it be out of ignorance, intolerance, or confusion, Wiccan are commonly the subject of harassment. The Wiccan religion has even been the subject of child custody cases often arguing against the parental rights of a Wiccan individual. There are some religious elements in the Wiccan religion that lack harmony with Christian teachings. Christians, Muslims, and Jews do not share a belief in Jesus as the son of God, but that does not stop people from having interfaith dialog. This does not seem to be the case with our Wiccan friends. Wiccans have great respect for the spiritual integrity of our planet and lift those elements up for praise. Using the Bible as weaponry and name-calling is deplorable and using Bible passages out of context does not lend itself to the nature of Christianity.

BEGONE HEATHENS

Sometimes those who refer to themselves as Christians use the phrase "Begone Heathens." For some reason they are confused by the differences between Atheism, Paganism, and Heathenism. Those who do not believe in any gods or goddesses are referred to as atheists. A heathen is an individual who applies pre-Christian or ancient Germanic religious practices. Heathens worship the Norse and Germanic goddesses and gods. Heathens believe in a polytheistic philosophy; that each goddess and god are distinct and real individuals not some concept of a greater power. Heathens take their religion seriously, as do Wiccans.

The main difference between Heathenism and Wicca is that Wiccans Worship Gods and Goddesses from cultures other than those of the Norse or Germanic. Both Wicca and Heathenism are modern day polytheistic practices that are rotting in pre-Christian philosophy. Both have a feeling of being strongly connected with the earth and all beings that share this world with humans. Both believe they interact with those deities they worship and that the deities are active in all things Earthly.

Wiccans and Heathens do not believe there has to be a special person(s) to contact the Gods for them. In traditional Wicca, everyone is initiated as priest or priestess. Heathens and Wiccans do have some specialized clergy, but they function in the role as teachers or advisers or organizers.

Another primary difference between the two is that Wiccans see their deities as aspects of the Great Goddess and of the Horned God, whereas Heathens see goddesses and gods as separate and unique individuals. There is a greater lack of polarity with Heathenism than in Wicca. Wiccans hold symbolic rituals regarding the union of athame and chalice (God and Goddess). Heathens do not practice this concept. Wiccans are much more centered around magical things with sacred spaces created for the invocation of Gods and Goddesses.

TRANSFORMATIONAL WICCAN SPIRITUAL PRACTICES

The religious landscape for the Wiccan entails a practice of transformation and change. It is an awareness of transformation and the cycles of change in nature and in the life of humans that is central to Wiccan spiritual practices. Witches draw upon their theology regarding the continuous cycles of nature celebrated by the eight seasonal holidays (sabbats) of the solar calendar and the phases of the moon's monthly lunar cycle. Both of these cycles are the foundation for the rituals practiced by Wiccans to celebrate and begin the transformation of the individual and the natural world. Wiccans have an acute awareness of their own creativity in bringing about transformation and change, such as the change of seasons, and devote themselves to the life-long practice of spiritual growth. Healing rituals are practiced as a transformational process from sickness to health.

Chapter Three:

THE WICCAN HOLIDAYS & FESTIVALS OF THE WHEELS OF THE YEAR

WHEEL OF THE YEAR SYMBOLIZING THE EIGHT RELIGIOUS NEO-PAGANISM AND THE WICCA RELIGIOUS celebrations, the Wheel of the Year Sabbats include four seasonal festivals which celebrate the changing seasons, and four solar festivals: Winter Solstice, Spring Equinox, Summer Solstice, Fall Equinox. Time was known as cyclical to the ancient Celtics; seasons change, and people came and died, but all was to return again in some form or another and the cycle naturally repeated itself. In present times the Wheel of the Year helps Wiccans to remain balanced in a world which is uncertain. The present-day Wheel of the year was first coined by Jacob Grimm in 1835, a scholarly mythologist, and became fixed by the Wicca movement in the 1950s. The holy days of the Wheel of the Year includes:

Name	Holiday	Earth Event	Date	Occasion
Samhain	Halloween	Fifteen Scorpio	October 31st	Cleaning and releasing. Celebrating the dead.
Yule	Christmas	Winter Solstice Capricorn	December 20-25	Song, fellowship, candlelight, and lighting the sacred fire.
Imbolc	Candlemas	Midway between the Winter Solstice and the Spring Equinox: Aquarius	February 1-2	Lunar Fire Festivals Day of Feast and celebration for the recovery of the Earth Goddess after giving birth.
Ostara	Easter	Spring Equinox Aries	March 20-23	Spring cleaning; planting seeds.
Beltane	May Day	Taurus	April 30-May 1	Fertility; Fire celebration. Couples dance around the fire.
Litha	Midsummer	Summer Solstice Gemini	June 20-22	Gratitude for life and light. Honors the Sun God.
Lughnasadh	First Harvest	Halfway between the summer solstice and autumn equinox Leo	August 1	Symbolic gifts of the first fruits given to priests as an offering to deity. Honoring hard work and that it pays off.
Mabon	Thanksgiving	Autumnal equinox Virgo	September 20-23	Time for resting after the hard work of the harvest. A time to reap what was sown. Time to finish up projects.

These eight holy festivals are constructed to bring attention to what each has gained and lost during the year. The Celts and other ancient civilizations believed that being ungrateful was a sin leading the sinner into the pit of darkness, resentment, bitterness, and self-pity. In order to have balance in life people need to take pause and reflect on what they are grateful for and cherish the memory of anything lost.

HALLOWEEN: SAMHAIN

The Sabbats corresponded to the time of year that the natural cycles of the seasons occur. Similar to New Year's Day, Samhain denotes the yearly cycle's beginning. The word Samhain means the end of summer. It marks the end of the Summer (season of light) and the beginning of the season of darkness. Now, darkness here has no negative connotation, does not mean anything evil or sad; there must be darkness to have light, so it is simply part of the human condition. At the Samhain festivals, thanks are given for the past year and reflections are made about loved ones passing on to the other side.

Many of the Samhain rituals resemble the modern-day festivities of Halloween in the United States. This is partly due to the recognition of Samhain being known as a time of 'in-between' where the dead can more easily move into the living realm. It is believed that the loved ones who have passed to the other side can visit during the Samhain, so it is traditional to prepare a feast and leave out goodies for the spirits of the dead. Witches who have wronged someone who has passed do not wear masks so they can be recognized when the spirits of the wronged come back seeking compensation. However, during the Samhain, wearing a mask or disguise was customary as a form of protection against the most potent powers of the spirits, fairies, and dead souls, who traveled at night and could abduct and seduce mortals.

Practices such as bonfires and other 'mischief night' activities are also traced back to Samhain. Paganism asserts that the world began as chaotic and that the divine forces created order. For this reason, it makes sense for Halloween pranks to symbolize this chaos and the rectification of these pranks on the next day shows the restoration of order. Similarly, bonfires symbolize light triumphing over darkness.

CHRISTMAS: YULE

Yule is the celebration of the Winter Solstice when the days start to grow longer. Ancient Pagans saw the Winter Solstice as the birth of the new sun god of the year. Traditionally, trees are considered to be sacred because they are home to spirits and deities. A decorated outdoor tree and gifts are given in honor of the sun god's birth. A bonfire accompanies the decorated tree as a symbol of new beginnings and the rebirth of the light. People gather around the burning Yule log and celebrate by singing songs and throwing a piece of holly into the fire to represent the past year's challenges. Each year a section of the Yule Log is kept to fire up the next year, symbolizing continuity.

Yule also represented the Oak King's triumph over the Holly King who was his brother. These two entities represented the changing seasons. The Oak King governed the earth by conquering the Holly King in the Winter and reins until the mid-summer with the coming of the Summer Solstice where the Holly King returns to battle the Oak King and becomes dominant during Yule. Wiccan tradition holds that the Holly King and the Oak King are dual characteristics of the Horned God. Each twin rules for half of the year. They battle each other to win favor of the Goddess, and then the loser retreats to care for his wounds for six months until he once again will rein the Earth.

CHRISTMAS: IMBOLC

Imbolc occurs at the middle point between the Winter Solstice and the Spring Equinox and is associated with fertility, hope, purification, and pregnancy. Imbolc from Old Irish means "in the belly" of a pregnant sheep. The Imbolc festival symbolizes a promising future and activities involve weaving dolls tributing the Celtic goddess Brigid from corn or wheat stalks to symbolize fertility, luck, and continuity. Brigid, the fertility goddess, looks to an early spring and is celebrated in the United States as Groundhog Day. Some Wiccan covenants change the date from the original February 1st holiday to one which corresponds to the coming of Spring in the area within which they live.

EASTER: OSTARA

Following Imbolc, Ostara celebrates the Spring Equinox. Celebrations for Ostara include many of the same themes as Easter: colored eggs, flowers, rabbits, baby chicks, and fancy feasts. The word Ostara stems from the Germanic goddess of fertility and spring, Eostre, meaning mother of the dawn. According to Wiccan tradition, the goddess comes back from beneath the earth where she lies in sleep for months until it is time to become pregnant with the next sun god born on each Yule. Renewal and rebirth are the emphasis of the Sabbat which is why the symbolization of the egg is important as is the concept of the labyrinth. The labyrinth dates back some 12,000 years ago to the Neolithic Age in areas as diverse as India, Greece, and Ireland. It symbolizes the aspect of dissociating from your own unique external reality in search of a greater meaning within yourself. This is portrayed possibly by the commonly practiced Easter Egg hunt. The ritual of hunting for a hidden egg elevates the person's consciousness to a new threshold.

MAY DAY: BELTANE

With the coming of summer begins the celebration of Beltane. As commonly used in other Wiccan festivals, bonfires play an important role. However, in this instance, the fire represents passion and putting aside inhibitions so one can indulge in their own desires. Beltane, meaning *bright fire*, also celebrates light and fertility. Dancing is an important aspect of the Beltane celebration, often circling around a tree in ancient days. Presently, a Maypole is constructed as a phallic symbol which is adorned with long ribbon strands held by participants as they dance around it. Beltane corresponds with Mayday which is celebrated throughout Europe. As dark days gave rise to increasing light, all of nature, including sprites, fairies, and other unseen entities awakened. During Beltane to ward off fairy spells and other mischievous activities conducted by fairies, pagans would perform cleansing rituals by carrying a lit candle to all four corners of the home, from front to back, and from side to side, connecting eight points of a protective invisible net to symbolize balance and harmony.

SUMMER SOLSTICE/MIDSUMMER: LITHA

Litha is in honor of the Summer Solstice and the longest day of the year. This is the day in June the

Holly King defeated his brother the Oak King and the days become shorter. The Litha festival involved feasting on fresh fruits and honey cakes, and dancing. Bonfires are set to protect people from forces unseen. It is a celebration of light over darkness and knowing that in the future darkness will overtake the light. Hence, longer nights and shorter days are only temporary and vice versa. Some people got married on Litha as part of its celebration. It was feared that newly awakened unseen entities were at their strongest by Litha and therefore could do one the most harm. Sun Wheels were made from corn and wheat stalks and rituals were performed for protection.

Witches can be very creative with Litha ritual ideas such as blessing water with magic to passionately grow their gardens and weaving abundance spells under the midsummer's night sky over their gardens. Litha is an inspiring day of brightness and inner power. It is not unusual for Wiccans to nestle into a quiet spot to meditate about the light and dark powers in the world. Some Wiccans follow more traditional rituals of fire, such as bonfire or a small fire in a pot in one's home. Others find Litha a perfect time to practice love magic!

FIRST HARVEST: LUGHNASADH

Lughnasadh is a harvest festival denoting the change from summer to autumn. It is named after the hero-god Lugh and is associated with truth and order. The harvest's first fruits were offered to the goddesses and gods. Lugh was an early Irish deity god of light and whose mother, Tailtiu, died from overworking herself, plowing and preparing the land. Lugh honored his mother's sacrifice by giving a yearly funeral feast which became known as Lughnasadh. Present day Wiccans throw festivities with competitions in archery, horse-racing, fencing matches, and foot races. Lughnasadh also acts as the final celebration before the end of summer.

THANKSGIVING: MABON

Mabon, labeled as recently as the 1970s, celebrates thanksgiving and thoughts about what has been gained and lost over the past year. It is a celebration of the Autumn Equinox. Mabon was named after the Welsh God who was a son of the Earth Mother Goddess. As a symbol of the second harvest, Wiccans may bring seasonal harvests, such as grapes and apples to an altar and then prepare a feast for friends and family. Apples commonly symbolized the second harvest. Rituals are conducted on Mabon to thank the goddesses and gods for a bountiful harvest and to celebrate an equal light day.

On Mabon, day and night are of equal length again; in perfect harmony; light and dark, feminine and masculine, outer and inner, balanced perfectly. But here lies the cusp of change as the beginning of the darkness, once again begins to conquer the light. The night will begin to lengthen and the days to cool and shorten. The trees' sap will head back to their roots, transforming the summer greens into the beautiful golds, yellows, oranges, and the fiery reds of autumn; returning us to the dark from where we came.

Mabon is a time of thanks to the diminishing Sun for the bountiful harvest provided to us. Each turn of the Wheel brings insights and other inner and outer gifts. It is also a time to rest after the hard work of harvest. It is time to finish projects, clear out what is no longer needed or wanted, and prepare for the winter descent and to look forward to aspirations of new hopes and ideas that will be nourished in the dark, awaiting for the return of Spring.

WICCA FIVE ELEMENTS

In the Wicca religion, four elements are associated with means and traits, as well as the directions on the compass in the northern hemisphere. Followers in the southern hemisphere should use the directions corresponding to the opposite. The elements are considered to be the watchtowers, and when casting a sacred circle are invoked for protection.

Air (Increase Psychic Power)

As the element of the east, Air is associated with the breath and soul of life. Air is the element of focus for magic related to wisdom, communication, and the mind. Air whisks away your problems, carries away strife, and transports positivity to those who are far away. Connected to the suite of swords on the tarot card, Air is symbolized by the colors white and yellow. Air is absolutely imperative to our survival, and is an ever-present element which surrounds us, but can't be seen. The sky, birds, mountains, wind, and oceans all represent the element Air. The Air Element is connected to the mind, divination, intellect, and communication.

Similar to the Water Element, the Air Element is about movement; it can easily travel around the world and cause quick changes. Without it we can't breathe and the seed cannot be scattered about giving rise to new life. The Air Element also has destructive characteristics in the form of extreme temperatures and storms such as tornadoes and hurricanes. However, when in the form of a mild breeze, the Air Element can be experienced as a calm and gentle whisper of reassurance from the God and Goddess.

Something to consider about the Air Element other than we are constantly breathing is that to truly relate to this iconic element you have to be conscious of your breathing. Therefore, breathing techniques can help you to get the most out of your magical connection with Air. So can taking a nature walk and noticing the feel of the Air moving over your skin. The benefits of fresh air are understated, so making time to spend outside and noticing how the clouds and trees move will satisfy a deeper connection with the Element. Burning incense during rituals involves Air as well as dancing. The direction of the Air can also be used to enhance certain spells.

Fire (Element of Change)

Fire is not necessarily needed for human survival as we did live without it over 100,000 years ago. Fire is possibly the most captivating of the Wiccan Elements, and yet if touched will cause harm to the body. It is an important Element for a comfortable and healthy existence. Fire allows us to cook our meals, keep us warm, and provide light after sunset. The Fire element is associated with illumination, strength, creativity, health, and is represented by the light of the Sun and stars, volcanoes, and deserts. It is constantly in motion while it maintains the health of the forests through cycles of burning and rebirth. The Fire Element demands much respect for anyone who wishes to use it. Fire is the only Element that cannot survive without another material to consume.

Bonfires are often created as part of Wiccan rituals, either by a coven or solo Witch. The sound of the crackling embers and viewing the sparks can bring on a meditative and calm state of mind. Similarly, gazing at the flame of a candle is a way to connect to the Fire Element on a smaller scale. Witches have been known to read the flame of a Fire for signs and visions, described by the way the fire moves and shapeshifts. Some Wiccan rituals use the Fire's ashes for witchcraft, but there are other ways to commune with the Element of Fire. Raising your body heat through dance or exercise or spending time under the Sun are ways to spiritually connect with this classical Element. Fire is represented in leadership, love, energy, and passion. Ritualistically, Fire can be used as magic in baking and for love spells. As it is the Element of transformation, Fire actually represents magic and is the most spiritual and physical of the four Elements.

Fire represents

- Energy
- Inspiration
- Love
- Passion

- Leadership

Water (Absorption, Purification & Wisdom)

As the most important Element for survival, Water is the most essential of the four Elements for without it, everything would die. With the differential gravitational pull of the Moon creating the tides, the Water Element affects all beings considering that 2/3rds of our bodies are water, this shapeshifting element is associated with dreams, psychic abilities, and emotions. Known for traveling the path of least resistance, Water flows easily about the world.

The Water Element takes many forms: ice, gas or steam, and collections after rain only to be reabsorbed by the Sun. It is associated with oceans, rivers, streams, ponds, and lakes, and benefits life with its healing, nourishing, cleansing, and purifying qualities. However, the Water Element is a powerful one and can be life-threatening when manifested in storms, tsunamis, and hurricanes through the interaction with other Elements. It can put out a fire, flood the ground, and corrode seashores and metal. However, in general, the Water Element is soothing to the human spirit.

Swimming in the ocean, lakes, rivers, ponds, and other natural bodies of Water is a wonderful way to connect with the Water Element. Spiritual connections are made by taking the time to reflect upon the way you feel while bathing, exercising, or meditating after your time with this classical Element. Playing in the swimming pool works too, as do baths and showers. Taking the time to honor the Element while you are drinking, taking a walk in a light rain, or just meditating to its sound will fill you with an appreciation for all things in life. Take notice of the many recordings and videos of waves, thunderstorms, and bubbling streams to feel the essence of this Element flowing throughout your life. Taking a ritual bath before conducting a spell, or celebrating Esbats, and Sabbats will enhance your magical powers.

Water Represents

- Emotions Sadness
- Joy
- Intuition
- Going with the flow of life.

Earth (Strength & Wealth)

The ever-present Earth is the foundation of all life. With its versatility and manifestation of both seed and soil and experienced in the eternal cycle of growth, harvest, decomposition, and rebirth, the Earth Element is strength. Earth and its great diverse features found in vases, gardens, valleys, fields, and forests is represented with prosperity and abundance in the form of trees used to build out shelter, and minerals we need to sustain our health. But the Earth Element has the power to destroy life in the form of earthquakes, avalanches, and landslides. The Earth Element has the power to balance our lives and keep us calm during the "peaks and valleys" which life has to offer.

One way to commune with the Earth Element is to appreciate and experience what it has to offer. Hiking, camping, and nature walks are ideal methods for connecting to this classical Element. Simply, taking a stroll through your neighborhood or a park works well too. A fantastic way to experience the grounding and healing energies of the Earth is to simply spend some time in your garden or just by taking your shoes off and feeling the ground. Laying and meditating in the grass or placing your hands up against a tree while taking in how the energy of the Earth can spiritually shift you into a place of stillness and ease. If you do not have a yard or outside area, such as in the case of apartment dwelling, potted plants, herbal gardens, or just using fresh root veggies can do the trick. When using a fresh vegetable, take the time to sense its rawness, smell its essence, and give thanks to the Earth Goddess for its generous bounty. Winter is its season, and its colors are brown, black, yellow, and green. Often before casting a sacred circle, the Earth

Element symbol is salt which is used to form the circumference. Soil can be used to clean and connect magical tools or can be added to certain spells.

Earth Represents

- Animal instincts
- Grounding
- Foundation
- Depression Vitality

Spirit (Well-being, Joy & Union)

Spirit, sometimes referred to as The Fifth Element, is also called Akasha or Aether. The Spirit Element bridges the gap between the spiritual world and the physical world. While the four classical Elements of Water, Fire, Air, and Earth combined make up the physical world, the Spirit Element exists in each one of them. While the Spirit is not a material, it is present and a part of everything else. It cannot be seen yet is essential for the balance and connectivity of all other Elements. The Spirit is what is summoned in rituals through the invocation of the Goddess and God, and of Earth, Wind, Fire, and Water. By recognizing the Spirit, and having focused and clear intent, this core energy can be used to create change through work with magic. It differs from the other four Elements, in that it is part of all that exists and therefore, does not have a specific ritual or correspondence with magic. Spirit can be associated with the color white and is not connected to any gender, season, direction, or energy type. It is represented by the Wheel of the Year and all magic in its entirety.

The Spirit Element is that of spiritual intelligence, hence it has no specific symbol. However, the pentacle is often thought of when discussing the Spirit Element because of the Star's five points (one for each of the Elements) which is surrounded by a circle which can represent the Spirit holding all of creation together.

In ancient Greek times, where the Western philosophy of the Elements started, it became clear to Aristotle and other philosophers that there was something more to the classical Elements and when it came to the universe, there was more than meets the eye. The term "Aether" was given by the Greek philosophers to the celestial air that the gods breathed. At first, it was thought to be a part of the Air Element but later it was realized to be an entity in its own right. Akasha is an Eastern aspect of the Spirit Element, meaning atmosphere or space. Space meaning not of physical form, present, yet unseen, from which all creation came. Whichever term is applied, the Fifth Element, Spirit, can be challenging to stay aware of in our noisy, busy world within which we live. That is why prayer and meditation, and rituals are important and treasured activities among all types of spiritual seekers. Coming to the altar, calm and still, to observe sacred rituals, it is easier to get back to this intangible and mysterious energy that is all-encompassing. The characteristics of Spirit are represented through ritual, magic, religion, music, art, and writing. It is nowhere and everywhere and unites and connects us to otherworldliness. It guides us past the narrow boundaries of the physical Earth and allows us to be open to something much more vast; going beyond emotion and thought. Even though it is invisible, its presence is greatly felt.

Spirit Represents

- Joy and Union
- Transcendence
- Transformation
- Change
- Everywhere and Nowhere
- Within and Without Immanence

Chapter Four:

THE OVERVIEW OF WICCAN COVENS, CIRCLES, SOLITARY PRACTICE & THE MAGIC OF THE WITCH

A BASIC COVEN IS A GATHERING OF A GROUP OF INITIATED WITCHES. EACH COVEN member specializes in a specific branch of magic, such as the harvest, healing, and love. According to the U.S. Census Bureau, Statistical Abstract of the United States (2011), approximately 1.5 million individuals, identify as Wicca. After studying the Wiccan religion for a year and a day, initiation puts the new Witch on the road to making things official. By joining a coven, the new Witch has the chance to become a high priest or high priestess, leading those with enough education, dedication, and experience to become a Wiccan coven leader. Coven meetings generally involve sabbats to celebrate the Wheel of the Year festivals, and esbats, which are non-sabbat meetings such as phases of the moon. The full moon appears once a month and lights up the sky, presenting a time for Wiccans to pay tribute to the Goddess. Esbats are thought to be the "second" Wheel of the Year and are the counterparts to seasonal changes known as Sabbats. Both Sabbats and Esbats focus the ritual on God and Goddess contributions to the circle of life found on Earth. During an Esbat, covens commune to hold rituals focusing on the Moon's relationship with the Triple Goddess. The Witches create magic under the Goddess's divine light. Solo-Witches also observe Esbats along with Wiccan all around the world who are worshiping the same celestial event.

Esbats and Sabbats celebrations vary greatly from coven to coven, Witch to Witch, and tradition to tradition. But the Goddess is always up front and center, in the form of one of her many aspects. When the moon is full and it is Springtime, Wiccans may focus the Esbat to honor the Maiden, during the Autumn and Winter, the Crone. Sometimes, covens may have a specific magical spell during the Full Moon ritual and choose a Goddess that is aligned with that goal, such as Aphrodite may be invoked for spells related to abundance. Ritual magic is often practiced at Esbats and sometimes they are the main event. Covens might be working to benefit one or more of their group members, for the community as a whole, or even for the whole world. Solo-Witches may work spells at the Full Moon ritual for more personal aspirations, or to cast bigger intentions for healing the environment or peace in the world. In general, magic at a Full Moon celebration is used to bring about positivity, joy, love, prosperity, and spiritual and physical wellbeing.

THE CIRCLE

Both man-made and natural describes the space utilized for Wiccan rituals. This is a good description because it evokes the spirituality that lies somewhere in between. The Wiccan Circle of magic ideally occurs in a naturalistic setting but can also happen indoors. It needs to be a sacred space that accommodates all members and provides a certain level of privacy. Witches unmake the sacred circle when the ritual is over even when it takes place outside. The Circle exists temporally for the duration of the ritual. While the Circle is in existence, it is dedicated to a specific rite, the ritual is then performed, and then the Circle is dismantled. A perfectly normal dining room may be temporarily transformed into a sacred place of worship, then once again returned to a typical dining room. No Circle is ever exactly the same. Witches may create the Circle ritual in the same place with the same casting many times, yet each casting ritual is completely unique. Quite interestingly, a Circle can be cast just about anywhere. The space within is considered to be a place between the Natural, realms of deities, and Human world. It is not of this world or otherworldly, it is a place fit for entrance of the Gods and a sacred place for the Gods and Goddesses to communicate with their followers.

By no means do Wiccans believe they are transported to another world, but the outer edges of the Circle mark the line between worlds that mandate different parts of the Witch's personality (Craft personality) and require different actions. When a Wiccan crosses the circumference of the Circle and steps inside, it is said that they leave their worries and fears behind and turn their attention to the deeds to be done within the Circle. The Witch is transformed into his or her sacred role which is acknowledged by using a Craft while in the Circle. In some respects, it is like the Witch's magical personality is revealed and all that that is authentic and sacred has been transformed from the mundane to the spiritual and back again every time a Circle is cast. Confidentiality about Wiccans, Witchcraft, and rituals is of authority by oath. After breaking the circle, a Witch is to leave the details and the identities of the members in confidence, as such the identities, exact wording, and specific details regarding ritualistic gestures will not be disclosed. However, the rituals discussed will be close in structure and in spirit to those experienced.

STEP BY STEP INSTRUCTION ON HOW TO CAST A CIRCLE

Step One: Using your mind, incense, or a broom to clean your space. Mentally you can push out, you can burn away with incense, or sweep away with a broom.

Step Two: After you have figured out how you want to clean you are ready to define your sacred circle. Consider your location and space carefully. It can be as small or large as you wish. You can mentally define your circle or use crystals or candles to mark the elements or directions. Use a cross pattern if mark The Earth, The Wind, Fire, and Water Elements or a pentacle for the Five Elements which include the Spirit.

Step Three: Begin by facing the east if casting a circle to call upon the elements. As you move clockwise, you will end up facing North where you can start your spell or ritual work.

Step Four: While standing in your circle focus on your breathing and begin to relax; take all of the time necessary to feel centered, present, and calm.

Step Five: Start to envision the Element, such as with Wind, that it is circling around you while saying "I call on you, Element of Air."

Step Six: Start moving clockwise toward the south and picture the flames crackling around you and the Sun's warming presence: "I call upon you, Element of Fire."

Step Seven: Start turning to the West picturing waterfalls, waves, streams; water flowing around your being "I call upon you, Element of Water."

Step Eight: Start turning to the North, imagining the Earth's fresh scent after a rainfall and how the cool soil feels under your feet. Envision the darkness of a cavern and the silence: "I call upon you Element of Earth."

Step Nine: While facing North, imagine your feet sending columns of light down deep into the Earth's core. Pull this energy to you from the Earth's center; into your being and picture a flowing white light, making the circle: "Under the Spirit, with these Elements, I cast protection circle within, below, and above." Here now you enact your meditations, spells, and rituals.

CIRCLE TIPS

If you need to leave your circle temporarily before the entire process, hold a wand or dagger by hand and create a cutting motion across the boundary of the circle: "I use this wand to open a door." Your wand will direct your energy to open a path. When you come back just do the same process in reverse to close the opening.

OPENING/CLOSING A CIRCLE

Facing the North, start the process with "Thank you Earth for your energy; Farewell. Opening or closing a circle is a method for thanking the Elements for helping you to release the energy you have built. Next facing West to release Water: "Thank you for your energy, Water; farewell." Turning to the South: "Thank you for your energy, Fire; farewell" and then face the East and release Air: "Thank you for your energy, Air; farewell." Ending with facing the North to release Spirit: "I bid you farewell, Spirit. I open this circle and send back into the ground the energy.

RUNE

Those seeking advice can turn to an oracle. The term rune means mystery. It is a system of reading utilized to gain insight or answers to questions or situations. Usually, runes are made of stone with a runic alphabet symbol inscribed on them. Elder Futhark is one of the oldest types of alphabets symbolized on runes. It features 24 runes, the first six spell out "futhark". The Old English or Anglo-Saxon version of runes were adapted making up the Anglo-Saxon Futhorc alphabet. Each rune symbolizes a letter of the alphabet and also has symbolic meanings. While very relevant today, many of the rune symbols are rooted in traditional meanings.

An example: Elder Futhark:

   F, Fehu: wealth and/or domestic cattle
   U, Uruz: wild ox.
   T, Thurisaz: a giant or thorn
   H, Hagalaz: hail or frozen pellets of water
   A, Ansuz: ancestral god
   R, Raidho: chariot or wagon
   K, Kenaz: torch or beacon

The Origin of Runes stems from an alphabet that was utilized by the Nordic and Germanic tribes of Scandinavia, Britain, and northern Europe for magical, writing, and divination purposes. Runic symbols have been found on weapons, stones, jewelry, and other objects dating back to the 3rd century AD, and probably were here long before that. The runes can assist you during problematic times and predict what is most likely to happen. They do not give exact answers or act as a type of fortune-telling, and they do not offer you advice. They do, however, offer suggestions on how to handle different variables if a situation does in fact occur. Runes offer simple hints towards answering your questions but leave it up to you to use your intuition and to work out the details. Readers of Runes know that the future isn't set in stone and each of us has the power to make our own decisions and follow our own unique path. Therefore, if there is uncertainty or you are uncomfortable with a reading, the power is within you to change your path. Runes can be used on many different occasions, especially in situations where you see an incomplete picture, or you have insufficient information.

Remember casing runes is not fortune-telling. Focus your unconscious and conscious minds on an issue that you are asking the questions about. This way, when casting the runes, they are subconscious choices that have been made, they do not fall randomly. Keep your questions or issues clearly in your mind when you cast your runes. Remember casing runes if for taking a look at potential causes and effects as well as noting their possible outcomes. You can make your runes out of stone, bones, crystals, wood, or metal; a simple set is all that is necessary. However, after practicing for a while and if you have developed a passion, then it is wonderful to buy or make a special set. There are many to choose from, so put your creative cap on and choose what you are drawn to such as carved stones or crystals. Whichever you choose, it's up to you; it is how you use them that matters. Most rune sets come with instructions telling you what each represents by its symbol and how to interpret them.

Runes are usually kept in small pouches with drawstrings to keep them together and clean or you can keep them in a decorated box. You would not want to lose one by accident. Make sure to have a rune cloth handy. It should be white and small so you can see the runes on them when reading. The cloth acts as a boundary for casting your runes and keeps them free of dirt or damage. It takes time to learn how to master the craft of rune reading. There are many guides, books, and online resources out there to help you to fathom runic meanings and the role they play in your life, and to the issues and questions you may want to explore. It is very helpful to be willing and open to using your intuition in revealing what the stones have to say. It is normal to at first not be sure. Write down your thoughts about any runes and see if their meanings come to you over time. If you cast a rune and it falls upside down on your cloth, that means there is a reverse or alternative definition. Even the most experienced rune casters can be unsure about a specific rune meaning but it suddenly comes to them at a later date. Some sets of runes have a blank one. But opinions vary widely on their validity. Traditionalists believe that there is no evidence historically that blank runes were ever used. It is up to the reader of the runes on how to proceed with a blank rune. You can include them or exclude them if that is what you are feeling at the time.

When it comes to reading your runes, start out in a quiet place, clearing your mind to focus on what you are about to read. Meditated on the question or issues and pray or call upon the spirits or elements to guide you. Have your rune cloth ready? There are many ways to cast your runes, similar to laying out tarot cards. However, on your first try, start by choosing one rune and accessing its significance. Once you are content with your progress, then move toward analyzing your casts and layouts.

The Three Rune Layout: Ideal for starters. Randomly pick three runes and place them on your cloth. Rune number one should be placed on the right, with number two in the middle, and number three on the left (3,2,1, order). Rune number 1 symbolizes an overview of your question or issue. Rune number two (the middle one) symbolizes a challenge. Rune number three symbolizes a potential course of action that you can take.

The Five Rune Layout: One at a time, select five runes and place them on your cloth in the following pattern: Number one goes in the middle, with the rest forming the shape of a cross around it. Place number two to the West (left) of the middle rune; number three to the north (top); rune number four to the south (bottom); and rune number five to the east (right). You can either place them face up and turn them over one at a time to read or conduct a straightaway face up reading. In this pattern, the three runes in position 2-5-1 (horizontal) symbolize your past, present and future. Ruin four (below the middle rune) identify what areas of the issue or the problem you are seeking answers to need to be accepted, and rune three (to the right of the middle rune) identifies what assistance you can receive that is related to your issue or problem.

The Nine Rune Cast: If you are trying to see where you are positioned in your spiritual journey and what is to come next, the magical number nine, according to Norse mythology, is the cast you can use to put to use your intuition. For the Nine Rune Cast, meditate on your spiritual wishes, and pick nine runes, randomly. Hold them in your hand for a minute or two and then scatter them around on your rune cloth. It is thought that the rune in the middle relates most to your current issues, situations, or questions. Those scattered around the edges are not as important. If the runes are touching, they may have influences that complement each other, but if they are on opposite sides, they may symbolize influences which are opposing. Focus your attention first on the runes that fell face up: jot them for reflection later. Then turn around the runes that fell upside down; keeping them in their same position, read them. These runes may symbolize future possibilities or outside influences.

GROUNDING

Earthing or Grounding power is a way to be personally connected to the energy of the Earth. When feeling anxious or stressed, grounding techniques are a great way to release any overloaded energy from within yourself. And, if you need energy, grounding techniques enable you to pull it from the Earth providing you with enough power while not exhausting your own supply. To begin, sit comfortably with your hands flat on the ground or lay flat on the ground. Breathe deeply three times while picturing energy flowing through you into the Earth or do the opposite if you are needing the energy. Keep visualizing the flow of the energy until to get the desired effect. Another technique is to envision yourself as a tree, deeply rooted into the ground, feeling the flowing energy through your spine.

CENTERING

Once feeling grounded, you may consider centering your energy. The center of your physical body is also your place of balance, your center of gravity. This place lies somewhere between your navel and your breastbone. You may also know if you have an energy center where you store your personal energy. If you need to locate it, picture something you love with great emotion, when you feel the emotion swell, pinpoint its area in your body; this is your center. Begin by putting yourself in the same position you used for grounding, and relax your physical, mental, and emotional awareness at the center of your body.

SHIELDING

To protect yourself from dangerous, depleting, or counter-productive energy, use the shielding technique; it's easy. Create a sphere or clear bubble of light surrounding your body. Imagine how it moves with you and protects you. Picture it as an actual shield and with great practice you can learn how to shield your home, car, or even your bed.

VISUALIZING

The ability to visualize something in your mind allows you to create a complete mental image of an event, person, place, or thing. You can visualize sounds, tastes, sights, and create tactile sensations in your mind. It is like experiencing your senses when you dream, only you are not asleep. Visualizing something in your mind makes it much more accessible. For instance, if you can see yourself as a successful writer, you are more likely to become one. Here are the steps for how to visualize:

1. Think about a time when you were content or happy.
2. With your eyes closed, breathe deeply.
3. Visualizer yourself at that happy time. Try to remember the scene, smell, sounds, tastes, and feelings.
4. Practice visualization right before you go to sleep and just after you wake up as these times enhance your ability to connect to your unconsciousness.

MEDITATING

Practicing meditation helps you to silence the busy chatter in your mind and access profound spiritualism and relaxation. There are numerous benefits to mediation, physically, emotionally, mentally, and spiritually. It can relieve pain and reduce stress, helping you to access your magical skills easier. Use mediation to increase your insight on how to communicate with Goddess and God, the Elements, and your inner Witch. Witches use meditation to clear their thinking and ready themselves for magic, ritual, and divination. There are two ways to meditate, concentration on a single mantra, your own breathing, or on a single image and mindful meditation which means being attuned with all and everything sacred. You can train your brain to recognize each and every thought, sense, and perception that passes through you with getting held up on a single one. Here is one way to use concentration meditation:

1. Wearing comfortable clothing, lay or sit comfortably with eyes closed.
2. Focus on your breathing, feeling the sensation of the air moving in and out.
3. Every time you begin to feel distracted, calmly redirect your thoughts without judging yourself for getting distracted.
4. Note: You can also use words, prayers, sounds, or whispers repetitively.

RELAXING

It is well known that anxiety and stress obstruct the flow of positive energy and take a terrible toll on your spiritual, physical, mental, and emotional health. They deteriorate the quality of life. Wiccans practice relaxation techniques to prepare for ritual as it helps to concentrate and focus on the task at hand. Again, breathing exercises come in handy for relaxing. Also, a good dose of muscle relaxation therapy will help take the tension out of a stressed-out body. While breathing in your nose and out of your mouth; deep breaths, concentrate on each muscle group or body part starting with your feet, moving up to your ankles, then your legs, abdomen, chest, arms, neck, and head. Do this for thirty minutes each day and you will notice a difference.

EXERCISING

Exercise can be a celebration of magic. Magic is carried out with the hope flourishing, not feeling small or shrunken. Witches can use exercise to deeply and physically connect with Spirit. It is a way for the body and magic to dance together in a sacred rhythm. It is a way to love your body and workout both your physical and spiritual fitness. Exercise, both physical and spiritual, enhances the quality of life. Rewarding magic and effective ritual takes concentration and stamina. If you are in good health, you can achieve a much more fulfilling practice in spiritual fitness. Yoga, aerobic exercises help you to manage your stress and protect you from becoming depressed and other emotional problems. Of course, you should check with an MD to develop the best exercise plan that fits your lifestyle, age, and any medical conditions.

One way to "get your magic on" is through what you wear when exercising. Wearing clothes you enjoy putting on that make you feel comfortable, will remove one distraction and make it easier to concentrate on your activity. Workout wear can be realized as ritual attire since you are dressing for an occasion, a ritual. This means choosing your magical colors. Maybe bright yellow gym clothes inspire your positivity, or black and red may draw upon your inner strength. Designs can be part of your ritual as well. As you progress in developing the best version of yourself, you may want to add to your ritual toolbox. Maybe adding gloves for your workout or special gym shoes. Nike gives some practitioners an added "swoosh" of magical incentive. Afterall, Nike was the winged victory Goddess. Clothes may want to listen to inspirational music while wearing earbuds as the sounds help them to delve more deeply into their ritual. Don't forget your water! There is magic in holding the cup or bottle and pouring energy, intent, and gratitude into the water. The gratitude is for its nourishment and cleansing attributes. Entering and leaving a sacred space in your exercise area is a way to open and close your ritual. This is the activity that begins the magical practice and defines the moment it ceases. All that matters is doing it with intent.

LIVING AND WELLNESS

Using the weekends to catch up on your sleep, means you are not getting enough of it. We have heard the saying "Don't underestimate a good night's sleep." Well, it's true. Not getting enough sleep hinders your concentration and focus and makes magical gratification more difficult to achieve. It also impairs your ability to drive safely and impairs your memory. It is impossible to maintain healthy spiritual and physical wellness without eating right. All of the practice in the world will not lead to success without proper nutrition. To the Wiccan, food is symbolic. With magic and ritual intentions for strength, love, healing, and prosperity can be achieved. This is the reason for food being consumed as sacred, therefore it is sacred in its preparation. Consider the following when preparing food:

- In figuring out which ingredients and preparations to be used, make sure to first construct your intention.
- Find out if there are mantras that will help you for your specific intentions.

- Keep your kitchen or cooking area spiritually and physically clean. You can use incense rituals.
- Chop your ingredients into symbols or magical shapes. Always stir corresponding to the sun's movement (clockwise).
- Concentrate on your intent in meal preparation. This will infuse into your food, positive energy.
- Strength and personal development can often be found with Wiccans who serve the community.

Witches believe, in general, that all is connected and come from and are integrated with Divine energy. The circle of life is connected by an energy manifested from Divination. Wiccan service is based on a shared belief in preserving the Earth's resources, ending poverty, preserving indigenous cultures, protecting nature and its animals, encouraging education and the arts, advocating for freedom of religion, practicing conflict resolution, and laughing. Laughing is therapeutic. It releases the natural antidepressants in the brain and elevates your mood. It is a spiritual way of celebrating joy, bliss, and delight.

HOW TO CONDUCT A NATURE RITUAL

1. Find a special place in Nature where you can meditate. The forest, by a lake, in a meadow, near the ocean, by a mountain, in a cave are all places to connect with the Elements and can be away from the company of humans.
2. Sit calmly noticing your surroundings and start to shift your focus from human centered to Nature awareness.
3. While meditating be reminded that you are a part of Nature and that you are there for Spiritual nutrition and to strengthen your connection to Nature.
4. Envision yourself being lovingly held by Mother Nature, as you feel the gentle Air caressing you as the Sky and Earth provide you with spiritual energy.
5. Express your thankfulness for the Cosmos, the Planet, and the Elements for their nurturance to all lifeforms.
6. Notice the life in all of the plants surrounding you and focus on just one of them. Touch, smell, and if you can taste it essence; essentially become the plant or one with the plant.
7. Return yourself to your human form and thank the plant for being a friend, a relative, a teacher.
8. Reflect on your spiritual time as a plant.

9. Next do the same with the environment surrounding that same plant and experience being part of nature.
10. Notice the sound of the Wind, birds, and animals.
11. Notice the colors, patterns, rhythms, and directions.
12. Take a mental picture of your spiritual sanctuary so you can visit it anytime while meditating.

PLANT MAGIC

Wiccans honor wild things and use materials provided by the Earth for their spells and rituals. In this way, they honor the Spirit Element. Plants have been around much longer than humans. It is safe to say that plants and herbs are part of the oldest known magical instruments. Prior to separating magic from medicine, healing was treated with herbal concoctions, ritual, and prayer. In present times, a simple cup of herbal tea can have a spiritual and emotional, as well as nutritional benefits. Plants symbolize the magical powers of the Elements. They start as seeds in the Earth, where they are nourished by the minerals and interact with sunlight or Fire Element. This in turn converts carbon dioxide into oxygen directly involving the Element of Air. Air in the form of wind and breezes gives way to more plant life with their stems and leaves which then scatters seeds to continue the cycle of life. All of which cannot occur without the Element Water. Plants are crucial in regulating the water cycles on Earth through purification and aiding the soils movement into the atmosphere. That is a perfect illustration of how Fire, Earth, Water, and Air are connected to the magical essence of plants. Plants can sense their surroundings and even communicate with other plants. Plant intelligence is the subject of much study these days. In natural and unnatural settings plants cooperate and communicate through their underground system of fungi and roots. They help one another by exchanging minerals and other nutrients and warn each other of impending dangers.

The science behind plant intelligence is a beautiful illustration of the wit inherent to Mother Earth. Wiccans tap into the magical energy of plants when incorporating herbs into their spells. That said, working with a garden is a great way to commune with Mother Earth. Growing your own flowers, berries, and herbs keep you in touch with the wind, rain, sun, and water, not to mention the role that animals and insects play in both life and death to continue the circle of life. When it comes to practicing magic, herbs are very useful and versatile. You can keep them in spell jars, sachets, and other charms used for your magical crafts.

ASH

Ashes symbolize transformation, change, and the union of Earth, Wind, Fire, and Water. Ash represents rebirth and strength. One of the great aspects of ash is that you can create it with endless combinations of ingredients. As with any material used in magic, holding it, wearing it in the form of jewelry, or sprinkling some on your altar will hold your spirited intentions. When gathering for Fire rituals to honor deities, offerings are ash can be handed out to each participant to tie everyone together during the celebration. Ash can be used for ointments, potions, and magical ink with which to pen in your Book of Shadows. Creating combinations of ingredients when sourcing your ash should have an inspirational meaning to you. It can be as simple as utilizing the ashes left from burning your incense or choosing your favorite smelling bark or wood with which to make ash. When creating your magic ash, consider your intent and what will enhance your ritual leading to more spiritual growth. Take care not to burn anything toxic to you or the environment. These items will be magically weak anyway. You can place under your pillow dried leaves turned to ash to stimulate prophetic dreams. Scatter the ash in all four corners of a room for protection. Wiccans commonly keep ash in a sachet to ward off negative energy. Carry it with you when you travel for safety.

BIRCH

The Birch tree, also referred to as the "White Lady of the Woods" is a symbol of great beauty and strength. Since it is one of the first trees in the spring to sprout new leaves, it has long been associated with rebirth. Considered to be a species of pioneers, Birch trees are the first to recuperate from fire burned land. Hence, there is a traditional association with new beginnings and fertility. In magical practice Birch is thought to inspire fertility, inception, and purification. It has antiseptic properties and is traditionally utilized for making the Witch's broom. The Birch spirit is said to offer protection and courage for those who may step outside of the safe and normal. Strips of Birch or Birch paper (so to speak) is a valuable tool used in witchcraft, so make sure if you buy it in a store that it is not an imitation. Birch has the fresh aspects of the Maiden, the Mother's generosity, and the wisdom of the Crone. It provides an abundance of positive energy and potency to magic. Use to meditate upon when starting a new project or invoke its spirit during any hardships for resilience.

You can pen your wishes onto paper made from Birch bark and then burn it to make them come true. Carry a piece of Birch in your pocket to protect you against fairy tricks and hexes. Use your Birch handled besom to sweep out dust and dirt from your home, so blessings can cascade in and your home can be purified. Putting up a piece of Birch tree over or near your front door will stop ill-wishes from entering. Make your magic wand from a piece of Birch for inspirational and protective spells.

CEDAR

Among some indigenous people and Wiccans Cedar is considered a sacred part of religious ceremony. The branches and leaves are steeped in tea or burned as incense to ready ritual space. Wiccans believe that Cedar creates harmony in emotions and prepares the mind for meditation. Cedar has medicinal purposes in that it functions as a disinfectant, lowers fevers, and calms a cold or flu. Because its wood doesn't decay it is considered too sacred to use as fuel for fire. Cedar is associated with longevity, growth, and power. It is used in making coffins because it doesn't dampen or decay and it repels insects. It is considered to be a psychic boost and when burned can attract money.

ELDER

The Lady Elkhorn or Elder tree symbolizes birth and death as well as beginnings and endings. The Elder tree is associated with the Crone as its magic gives advice on what to start and what to cast away. Elder has many benefits and medicinal purposes. It can be used as a pain and inflammation reliever and it is full of vitamin C. Making tea with its flowers can alleviate sore throats, help a cough, and help you to become regular. It is also great for kitchen witchery to be used magically in jams, syrups, and wines.

HAWTHORN

The hawthorn tree is known to Wiccans as a cleanser of negativity from the heart and inspires forgiveness and love. It represents the oppression of paganism and their celebrations by the Christian Church. The Hawthorn three is revered as the "tree of enchantment" and well protected by faeries. Its lovely flowers are thought to help prayers to reach the Goddesses and Gods. Folktales have it that if you, on May 1, are sitting under a Hawthorn tree, there is a good chance of being carried away to do good for the faerie world. Witches use the hawthorn blooms in spells for good luck while fishing, fertility, and happiness. Powerful wands are constructed from the Hawthorn tree and its blossoms are thought to be an aphrodisiac. Therefore, it is perfect for marriage and love spells. May Poles were originally constructed from Hawthorn trees. The magic of the Hawthorn wards of evil and Wiccans light candles on the Hawthorn tree at dusk on eve of May Day to welcome the coming of Summer. Having medicinal characteristics, the Hawthorn tree offers many remedies and brings happiness. However, caution is advised because of the Hawthorns--thorns! It is thought that the thorny crown worn by Jesus Christ was made from the twigs of the Hawthorn.

MAPLE

Maple trees symbolize love, longevity, promise, and the wisdom of balance. It is known for its magical sap or sugar which represents abundance and success. This may be due to Native Americans using Maple sugar for trade. It has both masculine and feminine energy. Its planetary associations are with Jupiter and the Moon and it is sacred to Virgos and Libras. The sacred bird of the Maple tree is the great horned owl. Many Witches use wands made of Maple for spiritual work. It is also considered the wood of the traveler because it enhances the acquisition of knowledge, intellect, and communication. Spells with the intentions of art, abundance, and beauty are often cast with Maple wood. It is a perfect wood for healing, purity, and cleansing spells. Hollowed out, it makes a lovely base for incense. It affords you the options for your path instead of having you rely on luck. Magic can be spawn by writing your desires on a special leaf you have picked out and placed in wax paper and sealed with an iron. Make a nice frame and hang it on the wall until the next autumn. Mulched Maple leaves added to your garden will bring successful growth for the coming year. And don't forget the Maple syrup!

OAK

Oaks trees have been around for some 85 million years. Oak is often used for making magically charged tools. Its leaves are used for sacred purification spells and rituals. Placing a sprig of Oak in your car, home, or office can promote prosperity, family unity, and protection. Oak acorns are used commonly for abundance of finances. Burning Oak brings healing and good health, and its ashes, carried in amulets increase fertility, attractiveness, and luck. It represents a balance of power and can provide strength and wisdom.

Magical Exercises with Oak

- One exercise involves tying two twigs of oak, with red thread, into the shape of a cross and then hanging it wherever you need protection from harm.

- It is thought that if you place a few acorns on a windowsill it will keep away a lightning strike.
- Wearing Oak in an amulet will keep negativity away and bring you creativity.
- On the night of a new moon, plant an acorn and abundance in your life will grow.
- Wear an Oak leaf near your heart and you can avoid being misled.
- Put two acorn caps in some very still water in a bowl and think about a love interest. If the caps pull together, it is a good match, if they drift apart, you may want to reconsider or that the timing may just not be right; you can always check again at a later time. Oak Wood fires can magically cleanse illness from a home. If outside it is said that if you catch an oak leaf falling from the tree, you will be safe from flu and colds in the Winter.

PINE

Pine symbolizes longevity because its leaves stay green year-round. Pine magically brings joy and good luck, so you can place pinecones around your home to ward off negativity and gain protection. Immortality, strength in adversity, making it through the tough times, and rebirth are all represented in the mighty Pine tree. The plant's resin is quick to burn and therefore symbolizes the Element Fire. Also, when burning its earthy scent is dispersed corresponding to the Air Element.

Even though the pinecones are considered the tree's womb, they represent masculinity and fertility, sometimes used to tip staves and wands. During Yule they are marvelous decorations in the form of wreaths and branches. Hanging a Pine branch in your welcome area will invite joyous energy and when hung over your bed will protect against illness. Pine branches can be used as a broom to sweep away negative energy out of your home or when placed on your altar will protect your ritual. The earthy scent of pine oil mixed with a bit of water can magically wash away your troubles or any negative entities disturbing you home. Mediating under the magical pine will award you with new perspectives.

ROWEN

Traditionally, the Rowan tree is most sacred, and in Scotland it can only be utilized for only sacred purposes; that means no using its timber or even cutting down the tree unless for ritual. Sacred to Brigid, the Celtic Goddess, Rowan represents, healing, smithing, and benefactor to the arts. Spinning wheels and weaving spindles were made of

Rowan traditionally in Ireland and Scotland. Also called the European Ash tree, Rowan trees are actually part of the rose family. Historically, Rowan trees were used to construct ship masts and various handles because of its thick density. It works wonderfully for a carving fashioned walking stick. Ancient ships were adorned with Rowan branches to help them avoid storms, as well as its branches being placed on the doorsteps of homes to ward off lighting. The Rowan tree has also protected the dead from hauntings when planted on the grave.

The magic aspects of the Rowan tree are one of the most sought-after wood species for the construction of wands and staves. Wiccans believe it helps them with their psychic skills and amazingly when the berries are removed from the stick there is the pentacle symbol where they were once attached. Its leaves, dried and ground create incenses magically used to invoke the Elements, Goddess, and spiritual guides, while the leaves are used in spells and love witchcraft. While meditating, Rowan essences help to open the mind and bring you more attuned to nature providing deeper insight as to the human aspect of the universe.

WILLOW

The enchanting Willow enhances magical abilities. It is part of the construction of the Besom. The Besom is usually made from three trees. Twigs of Birch make the broom and functions to rid evil spirits. Ash makes the stave for mystical protection, and the Birch twigs are tied together with Willow because they are most valuable for channeling the energy of the Earth, honoring Water, and locating lost items. The Scottish "Clootie" are springs or wells where strips of rags have been tied to the Willows for the purposes of healing rituals. When a Clootie or prayer rag is tied to the Willow, it is said to release grief. To have a wish come true, ask the Willow permission when tying a prayer rag to its branches. After the fulfillment of your wish, go back to the tree and with a friendly "thank you" untie the knot. In Celtic Tree Astrology, Willow falls on April 15th, to May 12th. It is ruled by the moon and anyone of the Willow sign is said to have many magical aspects of the lunar realm. Creativity, intelligence, and intuitiveness are all characteristics of the Willow sign. To conjure up the Elements and other spirits crush sandalwood and willow together and burn it outdoors at a waning moon. The smoke of burning Willow is thought to guide and sooth the souls of the deceased. It makes for a sacred meeting place for Witches as it wards off evil. It is believed if you knock three times on the trunk of a Willow tree evil will be averted.

YEW

The Yew tree is magically associated with rebirth/reincarnation, protection, and longevity. Referred to by Wiccans as "The Tree of Eternity," Yew wood has great strength. Sitting near a Yew tree is a wonderful way to communicate with your ancestors. Of all of the Earth's beings, the Yew tree is thought of as eternally alive. This is why it is highly valuable to spell works of longevity. The Yew tree lives so long because it can replace its parts anew and so is praised as a tree of rebirth. Many graveyards have Yew trees growing nearby. Some Wiccan practitioners are hesitant to utilize the Yew as its components are poisonous.

MAGICAL USES OF TREES

Type of Tree	Magical Use
Ash	Strength, harmony, skills, water, intellect and protect your home
Birch	Purification, protection, exorcism, cleansing smudge for the house
Cedar	Healing, spirituality, harmony, prosperity, purification, abundance
Elder	Protection, prosperity, sleep, exorcism, protection; must ask Elder tree permission three times
Hawthorn	Fertility, harmony, happiness, faeries, protection, otherworld
Maple	Love, longevity, money
Oak	Strength, fertility, courage, money, longevity
Pine	Immortality, healing, purification, fertility, exorcism, wealth, energy
Rowan	Divination, creativity, psychic powers, transformation, success, divination
Willow	Love, harmony, tranquility, transformation, intuition, healing, growth
Yew	Reincarnation, death, immortality, rebirth

MAGICAL USES OF FLOWERS

Flower	Magical Uses
Carnation	Strength, protection, healing
Daffodil	Luck, fertility, protection, love, exorcism
Gardenia	Peace, repelling strife, protection, love, friendship, healing
Hyacinth Iris	Peace of mind, insomnia, love, luck, Prosperity, averts nightmares, grief, pain relief in childbirth
Jasmine	Spiritual love, insomnia, prosperity, prophetic dreams, self-growth, innovation
Lavender	Love, protection, healing, sleep, purification, and peace
Rose	Divine love, friendships, peace, happiness, lasting relationships
Sunflower	Energy, power, protection, wisdom, wishes
Tulip	Love spells, protection, luck
Violet	Creativity, calming effect, prophetic visions, peace, tranquility, protection.

MAGICAL USES OF HERBS

Herbs	Magical Uses
Allspice	Healing, luck, money, energy, determination
Basil	Exorcism, wealth, love, sympathy, and protection, luck.
Cinnamon	Power, luck, Spirituality, healing, protection, love, strength, wealth
Dill	Money, lust, protection, luck
Ginger	Health, success, sexuality, confidence, sensuality, prosperity
Mint	Wealth, healing, energy, communication, vitality
Nutmeg	Prosperity, breaking hexes, bringing luck, protection
Parsley	Fertility, protection, anxiety, money, well-being, vitality, strength, quick recovery from illness.
Sage	Self-purification, grief, wisdom, improved mental ability, healing, spirituality, longevity, healing, wish spells, protection.
Yarrow	Marriage, healing, divination, banishment spells, anxiety, open mindedness

MAGICAL USES OF CRYSTALS AND GEMSTONES

Gemstones	Magical Uses
Agate	Connected Earth Element, matters of the mind, energy, mental health, discovery, truth, stress, depression, loneliness
Amethyst	Connected to the Water Element, Heliotrope, Zodiac Pisces and Aquarius, healing rituals, depression, anxiety, bipolar disorder, stress relief, intuition, cleansing, prevents overindulgence
Bloodstone	Connected to the Fire Element (Mars and Sun), healing, prosperity, fertility, blood health (heart, circulation, menstruation)
Calcite	Connected to the Water Element, Zodiac Taurus, enthusiasm, grounding, healing, joy, mars, money-drawing, moon, purification, success
Diamond	Connected to the Air and Fire elements, fertility, marriage, impotence, intuition, meditation, visions
Emerald	Connected to the Goddess, Taurus, conscious and subconscious, visualization, wealth, love, protection of children,
Fluorite	Connected to the Air and Water elements, Zodiac Pisces and Aquarius, clarity, crystal healing, chakra balancing
Garnet	Connected to the Fire Element, moon magic, menstruation, reproductive disorders, balance, spirituality, intuition, if taken deceptively there will be a curse upon the thief.
Jade	Connected to the Earth Element, truthfulness, serenity, love, innocence, liver, spleen, healing.
Malachite	Connected to the Earth and Water elements, powerful magic, transformation, purification, energy, peace, protection, success, love, warnings
Obsidian	Connected to the Fire Element, volcanos, antitoxin, energy, intuitiveness, subconsciousness, scrying
Pearl	Connected to the Water Element and the Moon, Zodiac Gemini, good and bad luck, protection, prosperity, calmness, spirituality, faith, loyalty, note: if a person believes in bad luck a pearl can certainly bring it because the oyster had to be killed to collect its treasure
Ruby	Connected to the Fire Element, Zodiac Cancer, guard against negativity, creativity, generosity, wisdom,
Sapphire	Connected to the Moon and Saturn, healing, inner peace, spirituality, Zodiac Virgo, intuition, memory, inspiration, protection, grounding, meditation
Tourmaline	Connected to the Water Element, Zodiac Leo, protection from negativity and demons, intuition, spells for self-confidence, personal power, rational thinking, and decision making, promoting a clear view of reality (through illusion and deception) and for spells related to revealing the cause of trouble, or the person at the root of it. Black tourmaline makes a wonderful scrying stone

Chapter Five:

INITIATION TECHNIQUES, FORMS OF WICCA & TYPES OF WITCHES

SOLITARY

MANY CURRENT WICCANS PREFER THE SOLO PRACTICE OF MAGIC. SOMETIMES IT IS because the individual feels they work better alone, and others may want to join a coven but cannot due to family obligations or geographical limitations. Both Solitaries and covens have benefits and if one is not working out, you can always make the change. Some of the Solitary benefits include moving at your own pace, making your own schedule, and not dealing with coven relationship dynamics. The downside is not having someone to share and/or gather your knowledge with. It is not difficult to put your studies aside when learning alone, so it is important to establish a daily routine that helps your move toward achieving your spiritual goals. This may include daily meditations, readings, and performing rituals. Keeping a journal or a Book of Shadows (BOS) of your magical studies allows you to chronicle what has and has not worked for you. Also, by documenting your spellwork, prayers, and rituals, you are laying down the foundation for your own tradition. It is a healthy exercise to look back upon and see how far you have come.

KITCHEN

Magical opportunities arise when taking the time to put together a meal for those you care about. Rather than dumping food out of a can; make it an infusion with magic ritual. Preparing food with your own two hands, lends itself to sacredness and can change the way you think, prepare, and consume a meal; you can practice magic here at the simplest level. The more you become attuned with what life is like to live magically, you may come to notice your kitchen is a magical place. Kitchen Witches commonly have an altar and a stovetop where they prepare their meals. Having a cauldron, candle, and maybe a statue of a hearth goddess can certainly add to the magically inspired ambiance. A display of your tradition including fresh herbs and fresh vegetables are of great importance to the Kitchen Witch. Other practices include keeping the sacred kitchen clean. Physical cleanliness supports spiritual cleanliness. There is no balance in clutter and chaos. Keep on hand your magical recipes in a special book, separate from your Book of Shadows. Consider stirring magic into your dishes with a widdershins (counterclockwise) or deosil (clockwise) direction.

Kitchen Witches use items normally found in the kitchen as magical tools and center themselves spiritually when cooking. Kitchen Witches enjoy using energies from the environment such as essential oils and everyday objects. The Witch infuses his or her own energies into their magical tools to use toward their intentions. They tend not to be overly concerned about a specific recipe and know how to improvise when necessary. Kitchen Witches tend to be passionate about their cooking and delight in trying new recipes and selecting ingredients based on their chemical properties or strictly use their intuitions. Special chants are often used to knead their energy into the final dish.

COSMIC

Cosmic Witches utilize celestial movements and planets in their magical works. Cosmic Witches feel unusually connected to the stars and an increase in their energy levels when working with them. Most Witches use elements of Cosmic Witchcraft as Wiccans honor the moon's cycles and star sign analysis to apply to their spellwork. The difference with the Cosmic Witch is that he or she focuses primarily on celestial events, planets, stars, and even celestial deities. Cosmic Witchcraft takes notice of the planets and stars locations and that allows them to know when and what type of magic can be worked in. Many Cosmic Witches begin with moon magic because it has several phases over the course of each month. Cosmic Witches pick the moon phase that speaks most to them and learn their potentials for use in their life and spellwork. Following placements of the planets and meteor showers are often celebrated by the Cosmic Witch. It is common for the Cosmic Witch to be well versed in tarot, Astrology, fortune telling (tasseomancy) and the study of bones (osteomancy). Many Cosmic Witches listen to celestial music and use it in their spellwork, but mostly for mediation.

GREEN

The Green Witch is known for their healing powers. Green Witches draw power and energy from nature in the form of herbs, stones, oils, gems, and other gifts naturally found on the Earth. Aligning with the name Green Witch is the workings with all things green. It makes sense to the Green Wiccan that if the earth is closely connected to the moon and therefore, the Green Witch tends to focus on lunar cycles. Using crystals, candles, and aromatherapy to support the magic of each moon phase, the Green Witch has everything they need to create a relaxing and rewarding spiritual journey. The Green Witch knows that humans have a strong impact on nature and often make their homes away from the hustle and bustle of city life. They believe you cannot be attuned with nature is surrounded by the noise of a busy life. Sensitive to environmental and animal ethics, the Green Witch senses the rhythms and cycles in nature and can feel the living, dying, and rebirth of all that is nature. The forest is the Green Witches sacred temple.

HEDGE

The Hedge Witch is named so because historically they lived behind the hedgerows along the outskirts of town. Hedge Witches served as healers and used plants and herbs they gathered by the hedgerows in their practice. Hedge witchery involves practices of green witchcraft that is heavily influenced by years of experience, folk customs, and trial and error. Like the Kitchen Witch, Hedge Witches see the kitchen and fireplace as sacred and magical places. Spending a great deal of time practicing herbal magic, the Hedge Witch's practice is deeply spiritual and personal. The Hedge Witch conducts all domestic tasks, whether big or small, from a spiritual perspective. Each meal is created with love and magical energy harnessed from the sacredness of the Earth. Hedge Witchcraft involves dialog with the home in the form of greetings, goodbyes, and a promise to return soon. Pomes, songs, and other gifts are offered to the home opening the Witch's spiritual life to the gifts and protection they have to offer if needed.

AUGURY WITCH

Augury Witchcraft involves interpreting signs in nature. Augury Witches believe that divine spirits live in everything in nature. Augurs interpret and study weather, cloud formations, eclipses, animal behavior, the actions of birds and all other aspects of nature. Similar in practice to a shaman, the Augury Witch analyzes symbols and signs in a person's life, not as a fortune teller, but to find out if the Goddess and God feel that the person is on the right path. They notice any appearances of animals which are sacred to the gods. They are prophetic Witches. In ancient times, Roman priests were called augurs and they interpreted auspices, which means the movement of animals and birds. They also interpreted the importance of lightning and thunder. If the signs fell to the right of the augur it was to be an ill-omen, and those to the east or right side meant a favorable outcome.

Augury Witches start their practice by examining their environment and the wildlife endemic to it. All of the Elements in that environment are important to survival. Flowers and trees are traditional mystic and magical symbols of divination, each with their own characteristics and qualitative. The Augury Witch then becomes oriented to the landscape which is as representative as the animals living there. Looking to the patterns of the terrain and the shape of the land tells the Witch much about themselves. To the Augury Witch, Nature's physical aspects are most important. The three most relevant signs are: the appearance of animals and birds, stones, furs, feathers, and the sounds, chatter, and calls of the animals; where they were heard, and which ones were most noticeable. Paying attention to fragrances and the cawing of birds on one day and sighting a species of tree anew to the Witch are all qualities that reflect an awakening to the Witch's spiritual path. They pay close attention to the colors of the birds, flowers, and energies experienced. Close attention is given to any numbers connected with the animals encountered as then can aid the Augur Witch in where to apply their energy. Notice is taken as to which direction any animals enter their experience, as well as the position (left or right, east or west, north or south), along with how they move in relation to the Witch. During an encounter with an animal, the Witch takes note of the kind of interaction including a lack of interaction. It is necessary to have studied the animal's normal behavior to ascertain the importance of any interaction. Finally, the Augur Witch asks Nature to talk with them by making a conscious action to be aligned with Nature. Sending prayers and thoughts through outdoor mediation asking Mother Nature for communication and signs and then patiently waiting for her answers.

CHARACTERISTICS OF DIRECTION

Direction	Characteristics of Direction
North	Abundance, balance, wisdom, knowledge, gentleness, appreciation, intuitiveness
East	Sun Element, rebirth, creativity, newness, healing, willpower
South	Change, transformation, protection, playfulness, trust
West	Visions, travel, dreams, spirituality, compassion, creativity

DRUID

Druid Witches practice magic based on the knowledge from ancient Earth, her stars, herbs, seasons, and primal wisdom. They are all about harmony, reverence, and connection to nature, so many are involved in environmentally friendliness. Druid ritual function to honor prehistoric ancestry. The Druid Witch employs aspects of the Spirit Element to summon protection for nature which is under attack from pollution. Many Druid Witches criticize the mainstream as exploiting the environment and worshiping technology. They feel a sense of belonging to the cosmic. The concept of Awen (Flowing-Spirit) inspires art and poetry. The word "Awen" is chanted aloud three times to involve the Flowing-Spirit, Awen. Awen in Welsh means "inspiration." Rather than covens, Druid groups are referred to as groves because it is a reflection of the trees, which is among the trees the Druids like to gather. Druid ritual is about aligning with the Spirit Element, and generally takes place in the daytime (in the Eye of the Sun). A circle is drawn, and the Wiccans begin hailing to the directions, and then mark out a space where the ritual will take place. Liquid offerings are poured to the ground, and often food items, such as cake, are passed around and taken. Following the consumption, a period of meditation takes place, and an energy from the Earth is visualized.

Afterword

Present day life is one of a fast-paced digital existence which can lead to a total disconnect from your spirituality and from the natural order of things. The aim of this book was to nourish your mind, spirit, and body by incorporating ancient philosophies and practices of one of the oldest religions known to man, Wicca. Wicca is the present-day belief in the union between nature, spirit, and being. It is not only a religion; it is a lifestyle. There are wiccans practicing from every cultural background, every religious background, of every ethnicity and sexual persuasion. Often misrepresented and misunderstood, Wicca is a beautiful way of life that promotes inner peace, a relationship with nature, and healthy ways to foster connections with the Elements and the world within which we live.

While there are many variances between Wicca and other Pagan religions, they share some common philosophies and practices. They both respect and love Nature and want to live harmoniously with the rest of the living and nonliving components in the World. Wiccans honor Nature's phases and cycles of life and death, and many Wiccans personally communicate and develop friendships with many lifeforms, such as plants, animals, and minerals. Rituals are an essential aspect of the Wicca religion, and often are conducted during Full and New Moons, and also at the eight Sabbats (seasonal festivals), which are spread out six weeks apart correlating with the Equinoxes, Solstices, and Cross Quarters (midpoints). Halloween or Samhain in the Wiccan New Year.

By reading this book you have hopefully learned how to practically apply ancient philosophies as a way to harness your inner magic to improve your confidence, happiness, and wellbeing. Frank Bawdoe has shared his in-depth understanding and education of paganism and the Wiccan culture so that the knowledge of how to passionately transform your life through enlightenment and spiritual connectedness is attainable. The Wiccan history was explained to provide a framework for the beginner Witch. Various rituals, spells, and affirmations were outlined so you can incorporate them into your life on a daily basis and create a positive environment to foster inner healing and spiritual growth. Each Element described shows you how to communicate and interpret nature and find strength and solace in the Elements. Natural remedies and healing are a huge component of practicing witchcraft and Wiccans have been doing the research for centuries. The ultimate goal of Wicca for Beginners is to empower you to find spiritual enlightenment, and how to focus and hone your mind to ways you can realize your aspirations while also finding spiritual harmony in all that you do and are.

I hope you enjoy this book as much as I loved writing it. If you do, it would be wonderful if you could take a short minute and leave a review on Amazon.com and Goodreads.com as soon as you can, as your kind feedback is much appreciated and so very important. Thank you.

Sources

Akasha & Eran (1996). Gardnerian Wicca: An Introduction. http://bichaunt.org/Gardnerian.html

Cunningham, S. (1988). Wicca: A guide for the solitary practitioner. St. Paul, Minn: Llewellyn Publications.

Gallagher, Eugene V.; Ashcraft, W. Michael (2006). Introduction to new and alternative religions in America. Westport, Conn.: Greenwood Press. p. 178. ISBN 978- 0-275-98713-8.

Guiley, R., & Guiley, R. (2008). The encyclopedia of witches, witchcraft, and wicca. New York, NY: Checkmark, an imprint of Infobase Publishing.

Hereditary Witchcraft. (n.d.). The Witch Book: The Encyclopedia of Witchcraft, Wicca, and Neo-paganism. https://encyclopedia2.thefreedictionary.com/Hereditary+Witchcraft

Horned God. (2002). The Witch Book: *The Encyclopedia of Witchcraft, Wicca, and Neo-paganism.* https://encyclopedia2.thefreedictionary.com/Horned+God

Lamond, Frederic (2004). Fifty Years of Wicca. Sutton Mallet, England: Green Magic. p. 63. ISBN 0-9547230-1-5.

Mitchell, Mandy. Hedgewitch Book of Days: Spells, Rituals, and Recipes for the Magical Year. Weiser Books, 2014.

Moura, Ann (2004). Green Witchcraft: Folk Magic, Fairy Lore & Herb Craft. Llewellyn Publications.

Murphy-Hiscock, A. (2009). The Way of the Hedge Witch: Rituals and Spells for Hearth and Home. Provenance Press.

Wigington, P. (2020). "The Rule of Three." *Learn Religions.* learnreligions.com/rule-of-three-2562822.-

Wigington, P. (2020). Eclectic Wicca. *Learn Religions.* learnreligions.com/eclectic-wicca-2562909.

Wright, G. (2015). "Brigid." *Mythopedia.* https://mythopedia.com/celtic-mythology/gods/brigid/.

Wright, Gregory (2020). "Morrigan." *Mythopedia*. https://mythopedia.com/celtic-mythology/gods/morrigan/.

Modern Witchcraft for Beginners

Your Complete Guide to Witches, Wicca, Spells, Ritual Magic, Divination, Coven, Traditional and Contemporary Paths

Introduction

Do you want to become a witch? Do you want to understand the history of witchcraft, the intricacies of the different paths the pagan world offers, and to delve into what it means to practice witchcraft in the modern world/age? Reading this book, you will learn the differences and similarities between Wicca and witchcraft and Paganism and witchcraft, the difference between solitary and coven witchcraft, and you'll understand the history and founding of the modern Wiccan religion and its influences. The Wiccan religion is dedicated to the betterment of humankind. To Wiccans, magic is real and exists on the Earth. Through modern-day witchcraft and ritual, tribute is paid to nature, the elements of Earth, Wind, Fire, Water, and Spirit and reverence is given to the two deities, the Moon Goddess and the Horned God.

In reading this book, I am looking forward to you gaining an understanding of the fundamentals of witchcraft and its many incarnations, what it means to choose the spiritual paths of God and Goddesses, along with ways to practice holidays and rituals.

Furthermore, I expect you to become familiar with the rich history of traditions based on ancient pagan beliefs, learn how to cast circles, and practice calling the quarters and elements.

As a devoted spiritualist, Frank Bawdoe shares a deep-rooted fascination with the philosophy of Wicca and Paganism. With a sincere desire to help all people, of all races, genders, ages, and cultural backgrounds to embrace spirituality, the magic of witchcraft, and to discover the divine within themselves, Frank is driven to ignite the flames of emotion in readers who are passionate about exploring the essence of life. Frank Bawdoe has authored numerous books on Wicca and Paganism, including *Wicca for Beginners* and *Witchcraft Religion & Spirituality and New Age Divination*. A passionate seeker of spiritual knowledge, Frank has explored paganism and Wicca in-depth with unwavering faith and dedication for truth.

In this book, Frank explores the history, theory, and practice of magic in the Wiccan and pagan cultures through the use of spells, meditation, visualization, and intuition, with the goal of transforming lives and finding harmony with the Universe.

Through magic comes serenity, a relationship with your higher-self, and an understanding of the common misconceptions about Wicca and witchcraft in general. You will be provided with accurate and up-to-date information about the fastest-growing religious practices in the world and learn common ritual tools used in magic, the different kinds of witches, and magic practices. You will learn how to craft your spells and rituals with several example spells provided. Learning divination and sigil magic is a way of infusing a pattern with magic that directs it in a prearranged way that can direct specific actions for those who know how to cast them properly. All magic is premised by the techniques of meditation and mindfulness.

Chapter One:

What Is Witchcraft?

Witchcraft is a nature-based, and vibrant practice in spirituality that is alive and kicking in our modern times, just as it has always been throughout history. It is also a topic of cosmic proportions that for those just starting out, can be overwhelming. There are many perspectives and much to learn about the best methods, techniques, and the correct ways to practice magic. This is one of the more complex studies of all forms of religion and spirituality. However, lighting some candles, buying some crystals, and burning midnight essential oils are only a few of the tools witches use on a regular basis when practicing their craft. Of course, you don't have to take my word for it because there are over a million Americans and almost 100,000 Britons currently practicing some form of paganism that you can ask!

There is a plethora of types of witchcraft and many choices for a new witch to pursue. Rather than overwhelming you with information, I think it's helpful to become familiar with some basic terms below:

Paganism: Paganism is an eclectic term for religious practices other than the Christian, Abrahamic, Islamic, and Judaic faiths that emphasizes the spiritual aspects of earth and nature. Neo-pagan is the term for modern-day practitioners who typically follow a spiritual path through life that is based on seasonal cycles, nature, and astronomical patterns. Some pagans refer to themselves as polytheists because they honor more than one deity. One of the many otherworldly paths falling under the representation of Paganism is the religion of Wicca.

Wicca: Wicca is a more popularized form of the neo-pagan religion attributed to a large degree to the named Father of Wicca, Gerald Gardner. During the mid-1900s, Gardner cultivated this form of paganism now known as Gardnerian Wicca. Whereas historically witches were usually thought of as only women, there are many men Wiccans who worship both goddesses and a god. Originally, Wicca was deemed as anti-monotheistic. It has recently come under scrutiny for favoring heterosexuality and the concept of a binary gender. This, in the 1970s led to the rise of Dianic Wicca, for witches who only want to worship the triple goddess and to only conduct rituals with other females. Since then, this particular train of thought was proven to be troublesome, due to many covens prohibiting transgender women.

Ceremonial: This is a practice followed to a T, or by-the-book, so to speak, where rituals, spell work, and ceremonies are executed according to traditional Gardnerian Wicca. Most often, ceremonial witchcraft is considered to be a highly preparatory and complex form of magic. The use of special occasion clothes, along with single-use tools fills a ceremonial atmosphere with passionate seriousness.

Brujería: Brujería is an umbrella term witchcraft practiced by Caribbean, African, and indigenous Latin Americans, with a history going back thousands of years. The word bruja is Spanish for witch.

Solitary: These witches have chosen not to participate in a coven, but rather operate on their own mix or type of witchcraft of their choice.

Eclecticism: These witches have chosen a more social path and have chosen not to adhere to a specific category of witchcraft but instead use a variety of traditional methods.

Initiation: This is a group of rites that put newbie witches on their path to becoming official witches. They usually accomplish this rite of passage by joining a particular coven and learning its traditions and practices for the ceremonial year and a day. With enough dedication, experience, and knowledge, these initiates have the opportunity to become a high priest or high priestess, or the leader of a Wiccan coven.

Coven: A community or gathering of witches who have been already initiated and are led by a high priestess or high priest. In the Wiccan religion, witches usually meet during Sabbats, which are celebrations known as the Wheel of the Year, and also at Esbats, which is in observation of a full moon.

Wicca and Witchcraft Origin

Wicca was a coven-based religion that developed in England in the early 1900s. Its religious exercises were primarily based on the texts of witch groups, such as that of Margaret Murry and other traditional British Wiccans. One of history's most infamous Wiccans was born in England in 1884 and was called Gerald Gardner. Gardner was an ardent follower of a witch known as Aleister Crowley, and was a member of a witch group called the New Forest Coven. Gardner then went on to become the founder of the modern-day religion of Wicca. By the middle of 1950, Gardnerian Wicca practices spread throughout Great Britain, Australia, and the United States.

Gardner learned his practice while he was working in Asia. Just prior to WWII, he went back to England and got involved in the local occult community. It was Gardner's Wiccan philosophy that led to people changing the way they thought about witchcraft into a positive perception. Prior to that, witchcraft was often perceived as satanic devil-worshipping and barbary. Before this time witches were only thought to be women. If a woman stood out because of being sexual, intelligent, or independent, she was accused of witchery, and many women were burned at the stake. If a man was ever associated with witchcraft, he was thought to be homosexual and flamboyant.

Modern Wicca vs. Traditional British Wicca

British Traditional Wicca, much like Gardnerian Wicca, operates as an initiatory mystery cult; membership is gained only through initiation by a Wiccan High Priestess or High Priest. Any valid line of initiatory descent can be traced all the way back to Gerald Gardner and through him back to the New Forest coven. Coven and ritual ceremonies are kept secret from outsiders and many witches of the Wiccan faith choose to keep their membership in the religion a secret. Individual witches decide whether they want to be open or keep their religious affiliation a secret, usually in consideration of where they live, their circumstances in life, and their careers. In every instance, traditional British Wicca strictly forbids any member from sharing personal information and someone's membership status without the complicit consent of that member, for each and every specific time of sharing. This is done for the protection of that member from harassment, and other heinous acts that may be committed against them. Like those who keep their sexuality closeted, Wiccans often talk about coming out of the "broom" closet. In traditional British Wicca, Alexandrian Wicca, and Gardnerian Wicca, there are three types of initiation which seem to be based upon the Freemasonry's three grades: Theology, Ethics and Morality, and the Return of Three.

Gardnerian Wicca Theology

There are two main deities in Traditional British Wicca (TBW), the Mother Goddess and the Horned God. It is a dualistic view of divinity, with God and Goddess regarded as opposite, yet equal celestial forces. A shared core belief held by most Wiccans is the practice and acceptance of ritual and magic. Similar to the viewpoint of Aleister Crowley, Wicca defines magic as the art and science of effecting change to happen in accordance to will. Wiccans believe magic is as natural as nature itself; a manifestation of transformation, not supernatural, that involves a combination of meditation, invocations, music, movement, and tools.

Wiccans use magic as a tool to enact upon a quantum or energy level of reality. The quantity of energy makes the decision about which direction reality will take.

Alexandrian Wicca

Alexandrian Wicca, named after Alex Sanders, was grounded in Gardnerian Wiccan philosophy. In the 1960s, Alex and his wife, Maxine, began their own branch of Wiccan religion, Alexandrian Wicca. Before a member is initiated, it is decided by the members of the coven as to whether the individual would be a good fit to their coven by gathering in an open ritual to interview the initiate. If accepted, an official offer to join the coven is made, and once the initiate accepts that offer, they start the first phase of initiation without being bound by the coven's vows. This phase usually lasts about a year, during which the initiate is exposed to the elders and the coven. The decision is traditionally made by the matriarchal representative, a high priestess. Once welcomed into the coven, the initiate then makes the decision whether to commit themselves toward a more serious journey, which is achieving the first degree of initiation. As a first-degree initiate, the new coven member needs to exhibit dedication and commitment to learning the craft with great enthusiasm. In the traditions of the Alexandrian Wiccans, every member is a priest or priestess. There are no lay people in this Wicca version; all coven members possess the ability to commune in fellowship with the Divine.

Wiccan Ethics and Morality

Traditional Gardnerian Wicca follows a core guideline of ethics known as "The Wiccan Rede." In a manner of the archaism still presiding in Gardnerian lore, "As it harms none, do as thou wilt," or in modern terms, when using magic, it can never be to cause anyone harm, unless it is to prevent a greater harm. The meaning of the word Rede is "counsel" or "advice." The counsel to harm no one carries equal weight as doing as you will. Therefore, Traditional British Wicca stands strongly against any form or coercion and strongly advocates informed consent. It forbids witches from proselytizing others and requires that anyone who wants to be initiated into the Wiccan religion does so through study, teachings, and requests to be initiated.

The guideline of Wiccan ethics is known as the Rule of Three or the Law of Return. This ethical guideline advocates that any positive or negative energy a person puts forth in the world will be returned to that person three-fold. This ethical boundary exhibits the importance of harming no one, for that would give rise to a harmful reaction back on oneself or on one's coven. These traditional Wiccan teachings inspire thought before action, especially when it comes to spell work. The coven and individual witches adhere to these guidelines as to consider beforehand what possible consequences may come from any magical workings. With respect to these ethical guidelines, it is safe to say that Traditional British, Gardnerian, or Alexandrian Wiccans hold themselves to high ethical standards. For example, the Bricket Wood coven was noted for having many members from intellectual and academic backgrounds and contributing to the preservation of Wicca traditions and practice. Gardner actively participated in disseminating academic resources regarding the occult and Wiccan folklore to the general public by opening his Museum of Witchcraft located on the Isle of Man. Traditional British Wicca differs from some modern-day magical practices that tend to concentrate more on the practitioner's spiritual development.

Common Myths and Misconceptions

Wicca was legally recognized as a legitimate religion by the Court of Appeals in 1986. However, Wicca is still a widely misunderstood practice and its members are misunderstood as well. Many modern-day witches chose to carry the title of Wiccans because the term "witch" still carries such a negative and evil connotation. One of those commonly misconceived conceptions is that Witches cast spells to harm or curse people. Loosely based on the rites and rituals of paganism hundreds of years ago, the focal point of Wicca is to give reverence to the seasons, magic, and the harvests. The government of the United States of America has ruled Wicca as an official religion, thereby making its holidays federally observed. However, they do vary according to state. In New Jersey, for example, eight Wiccan holidays are celebrated and recognized by the New Jersey Department of Education, allowing Wiccan children to be excused from classes on those days. Wiccans are entitled to the same rights as any other group.

Another big misconception regarding Wiccans is that they are devil worshipers, when in fact, they do not even believe in the idea of Satan. Concepts such as hell and heaven have never been part of the Wicca religion. Wiccans believe in goddesses and gods, not a single God, which is not that different from Buddhism and Hinduism. Likewise, animal sacrifices are a commonly held misconception about the religion of Wicca. Wicca is a nature-based religion and its members have nothing but respect for all living things. Sacrifices offered to Wiccan deities are given in the form of bread, flowers, fruit, or wine. There is no form of blood sacrifice in the Wiccan religion. Many Wiccans are animal lovers and animal activists.

Wiccans do not follow the writings of the Holy Bible, but they have created and handed down a Book of Shadows (BoS) to use only as a reference book. Wiccans are also known to keep magical grimoires (diaries), where they keep and record useful knowledge for practicing their spell work, rituals, and ceremonies. Magic is considered to be a natural activity in life, and Wiccans believe spell work is natural and should be used for various acts of good, healing, personal growth, and prosperity.

Also a misconception regarding Wiccans is that they are sexually perverse. While they consider themselves to be liberal and non-judgmental in regard to sexuality, it doesn't mean they engage in orgies or bestiality. Wiccan do consider gossiping about who is having sex with whom as trivial, unimportant, and a total waste of time. The only thing that really matters to most Wiccans is informed consent. A person's sexual preference, be it homosexuality, bisexuality, heterosexuality, or pansexuality, is of no interest to Wiccans.

Another common misconception about Wicca is that all witches are female. It is undeniable that the origin of the legacy of witches is based on women, which is because its history has been perpetuated by the demonization of witches and witchcraft to begin with. Witches are like everyone else, they come in all shapes, sizes, colors, genders, forms, ethnicities, and races. Historically, Witches were women who were persecuted for any semblance to witchcraft, while men who practiced spell work were revered as magicians and sorcerers. Witches were considered threatening to the patriarchal society because they didn't conform to societal and gender norms.

Contrary to some beliefs, people are not born witches. You sometimes hear about some attention-seeking individuals insisting they were born a witch. This can't be true. Magical ancestry is a powerful influence but it has no bearing on whether or not someone is a witch. There are very real aspects of witchcraft. Curses and hexes are real, which is in part the reasoning behind the Rule of Three. However, this rule also applies to positive magic. Hexes are primarily a black magic practice. While many consider white magic to be good, magic is neither evil nor good, it simply is magic, a tool used in spiritual expression. You definitely do not have to have years of training and initiations from confirmed witches in order to cast a spell. To do it, you don't need a full moon, animal bones, or a coven to enact spells. You simply need to put forth your intention and then perform a ritual to manifest that intention, be it a candle lighting ceremony, meditation, or some other form of magical expression.

You can write a letter to yourself with affirmations that you are special and loved and that you honor the Goddesses, God, or deity of your choosing to be practicing magic. Write a gratitude list and make a repeating chant out of it and you are practicing magic by harnessing positive energy; you are casting a spell. You don't have to have a lot of money to do this; magic is not an expensive practice and now that it is seeing a rise in popularity, it has become more accessible than ever. The myth that it is demonic and evil is increasingly being exposed. However, let me issue a healthy warning here. The witchcraft industry is becoming a big money industry, with many scammers looking to cash in on the incense, candle, crystal, and essential oil market. All you need to be successful in spell work is you! You have the power and the energy to make magic; this is never found in an item. You need not belong to a coven because you may prefer to "fly solo." There are also eclectic groups and other less governed witch groups who practice their craft in a more casual setting than covens with highly organized initiation processes. Every person's spiritual journey is unique and personal, so it is really up to you if you want to join a coven.

Eclectic Wicca

Eclectic Wicca is an all-purpose form of modern Wiccan practice that doesn't fit into any distinctive category. Many solitary witches choose an eclectic path; however, there are covens who identify themselves as eclectic. An individual witch or a coven may identify as eclectic for various reasons including:

- Mixed traditions: A solitary witch or a coven may use a mixture of practices and beliefs from several different traditions and pantheons.
- Modified traditions: A group can be an extension of a traditional established branch or Wicca, such as Alexandrian or Gardnerian, but has been modified in its practices, which makes it very different from the original Wicca tradition.
- Individual and unique forms of practice: A person can create their own tradition of practices and beliefs. Because this form cannot be defined as something specific, it is defined as eclectic.
- Uninitiated witches: A solitary witch may be practicing their craft by what they have learned from sources available to the public regarding Wicca, but not be using initiatory, oathbound materials; hence, their practice is eclectic.

Because there is often confusion about who is and isn't Wiccan, there can be disagreement regarding existing ancestral Wiccan traditions, and modern eclectic traditions. Some would say that covens based on traditional Wicca should be allowed to identify themselves as Wiccan. If we take that reasoning into account, any coven or individual who identifies as eclectic is not Wiccan, by definition, but Neo Wiccan. "Neo Wiccan" is not an insulting or derogatory term, it simply means practicing a new form of Wicca.

Dianic Wicca

Dianic Wicca started from the feminist movement and was founded by Zsuzsanna Budapest, a hereditary witch. Dianic Wiccans pay very little attention to the Horned God and focus primarily on the Goddess. Hence, most of their covens are exclusively female. A few, yet far between, have welcomed males into their group. In some area, Dianic covens have been stereotyped as lesbian witches, but that is not the case.

While most Wiccan sectors follow a system of beliefs that limit cursing, hexing, or negative magic, Dianic Wiccans are the exception to the rule. The Wiccan author, Budapest, is a known feminist who has argued that binding or hexing those who commit harm to women is acceptable. She calls for, in particular, binding and hexing of any men who have perpetrated violence against women and children. Dianic covens are self-identified, so it is known that their beliefs are Goddess-base, and that they are spiritually focused on feminism. They do celebrate the Wheel of the Year.

Seax/Saxon Wicca

Saxon Witchcraft, also known as Seax-Wicca is a modern Pagan Witchcraft, largely influenced by traditional Anglo-Saxon Paganism during the Early Middle Ages, between the 5th and 10th centuries. It was founded by Raymond Buckland, a Gardnerian Wicca High Priest born in England in 1934, who then moved to the United States. He had expressed his disquiet about the egotistical, corrupt, and abusive nature of some of the covens he witnessed. To address those concerns, he developed Seax-Wicca. He wrote one of the first books, entitled *The Tree*, that explored solitary modern Witchcraft and offered seekers a way to introduce them to a modern Saxon Witchcraft that could either be practiced in a coven or alone. Seax-Wiccans usually honor Freya and Woden, who are Germanic deities, and the eight Sabbats. They use the usual ritual tools, including a spear, and hold rune magic in high regard.

Celtic/Druidic Wicca

When they hear the word Druid, most people picture old men wearing robes with long white beards frolicking around Stonehenge. However, Neopagan Druidry is a religious philosophy about the ways of living life; while founded in ancient soil, it reaches for the stars. Of all the differences that a Wiccan has with a Druid, this is probably the most prevalent. In Druidism, there is no "Rede." In fact, the only people that the Rede pertains to are those who adhere to it; it is unique to Wiccans and some kinds of witchcraft.

Most Wiccans believe in the adage of "do as you will as long as you don't harm anyone in the process." Some Druids disagree that this ethical guideline has anything to do with them. Some Wiccans even accuse Druids of lacking ethics. However, this is certainly not the case. In fact, the moral virtues within the Rede and the Law of Returns actually imbue Druidism. Normally, Druids refer to this as Celtic Virtues. In general, these morals are described as Honesty, Honor, Justice, Courage, Hospitality, and Loyalty. These are the six principles of Druidic ritual and thought. To put it briefly, the morality of Honor requires one to hold true to their oaths and to do the right thing, even if that means hurting someone else in the process. Druids are obliged to stay true to family, leaders, and friends, defining their virtue of Loyalty. Druids also feel a sense of obligations toward being a good host when visited by friends or family, defining the virtue of Hospitality. Telling the whole truth to your Gods and your fellows adheres to the virtue of Honesty. Druids understand that every individual has inherent worth and that to hurt that worth demands consequences in some form or another. Courage, according to Druidism, means standing strong in the face of adversity alone or with companions.

Outside of the six virtues, pretty much anything goes. The Justice virtue holds you accountable for any harm to others and any good things you do; it's just. It recognizes the divine in each and every one of us. It is a commitment to do good. It is very similar to the Buddhist and Hindu concept of karma. However, this concept has not been part of European thought. The Celts have a history of functioning as an isolated tribal community. The Celts believed in independence as a supreme right, and fiercely demanded that right to be proudly honored.

Shamanism

Shamanism is a spiritual practice where the Shaman (practitioner) interacts with the spirit realm through higher states of consciousness, such as meditation and trance. The Shaman's goal is often to direct spiritual energies or spirits, usually for healing purposes, into the physical world. Shamanism is not an organized religion, but more of a spiritual practice that cuts across all creeds and faiths, delving into deep aspects of ancestral memory. As a primitive faith-based belief system, it was practiced long before established religion. It has its own cosmology and symbolism, inhabited by totems, beings, and gods who share similar characteristics, while depending on their set origins, appear in various forms.

Shamanism has been practiced and studied in cultures around the globe since the times of ancient people up to the modern day. The shamans' work is adaptable and practical and has coexisted over thousands of years with varying systems of government, organized religions, and cultures. Formalized religions, from Christianity to Buddhism, are rooted in ancient shamanism and still carry the shamanic traits of a strong connection to the divine in all things. However, shamanism itself is not a formal ideology or belief system, but a group of experiences and practices shared by shamans around the world in every culture. These adaptable practices coexist with different governmental systems, organized religions, and various cultures.

Nowadays, shamanism is practiced and studied as a life path. Following the perspective of shamanism, people look to be in a relationship with the spiritual aspect in all things. They find guidance and information for alternative realities for their own experiences in life, intentionally. Shamanism doesn't inherently contradict the practice of religion that allows an individual to be directly involved with whatever they choose as a power greater than themselves. Today, as was in ancient times, people consult with Shamans for pragmatic and practical solutions to everyday problems, including healing illness, family discord, career challenges, and ancestral issues.

Shamans practice in enraptured or elated trance states, voluntarily, which transforms their consciousness for astral travel through the invisible realms. The ability to effect changes and gather information in the spiritual worlds depends greatly on the relationships they develop while working with the spirits there. Hence, it is a relationship-based activity that affects changes in the spiritual realms to foster healing of many types in the physical realm. In some areas, Shamanism is an active part of the dominant culture, and for others it directly contradicts the dominant culture. Some people's intuitions lead them to seek help from a shaman. For others, it is a last resort when they have run out of options; often, they don't even know anything about Shamanism.

Shamans have the ability to:

- Alter their state of consciousness at will and control themselves when entering and moving in and out of alternate states.
- Act as mediators between the needs of the physical world and the spirit worlds in ways understandable and useful to the community.
- Serve the needs of the people in ways that practitioners of other disciplines, such as priests, political leaders, psychiatrists, and physicians cannot.

Categories of healers

1. Traditional shamans
2. Shamans that bridge traditional shamanism and Western culture, often by adding rituals and ceremonies that didn't necessarily come from their culture of origin.
3. Shamans called by the Divine to serve as shamans for the needs of the community, even if they were separated long ago from their original shamanic roots.

People seek shamans for healing many different ailments. If a person lives in a shamanic culture, going to a shaman for healing is usually part of a team approach, where the shaman partners up with nutritionists, physical healers, herbal practitioners, and other medical practitioners. In the Western world, shaman healing is usually rare. However, seeking contemporary shamans for health reasons is on the rise, especially for those who are not making progress with conventional approaches.

Animism

First defined in 1871, animism is the concept that all things, inanimate and animate, possess an essence or spirit. Animism is a key component in many indigenous tribes' beliefs and ancient religions. It is the foundational characteristic of ancient spiritualism and is recognized in various forms throughout many modern religions worldwide. Animism is the concept that all things are connected by a spirit. These include people, objects, natural phenomena, animals, and geographic features. Today, animism is often used to discuss various systems of belief in anthropological terms.

Animists hold that all life is of spirit, not matter. Humans, animals, plants, rocks, mountains, oceans, and so on, all have souls. All are good or evil, but the relevant characteristic is not morality; it is power. Spirits or souls are living things with moods, volition, and the capacity to harm or to help. Those spirits that are not inhabiting a living thing exist in the form of angels, Goddesses, Gods, energy forces, and ghosts. To the animist, all events on earth have spiritual causes. Spirits influence either the disaster or the success of human beings. Many spirits can be vindictive or easily offended. Others can feel threatened and therefore have to defend themselves by causing harm to humans. When spirits are upset, they throw life off balance and cause all types of troubles, from hurricanes to headaches.

For these reasons, humans have shown deep respect to spirits throughout history through customs, rituals, and offerings. Pacifying spirits yields blessings and restores balance. If relationships with spirits are cultivated, they can be powerful allies against malicious beings. To animists, a community consists not only of the living, but also the unborn, a totem, and the deceased family members. A totem is usually a plant or animal that gains its life-source from the same as humans within the same community. Conception, birth, and death do not define the sentient state of a person, but are different states of a never-ending existence.

Alchemy

Alchemy is an ancient practice wrapped in secrecy and mystery. The practitioners of Alchemy were on a mission to manifest lead into gold, but their aspirations went far past merely creating some nuggets of gold. Their pursuits have excited the imagination of people for millennia! Alchemy was grounded in a spiritual and complex worldview. They thought that all things contain a spirit that is universal. Metals that grow in the earth were thought to be alive. When a common metal such as lead was discovered, it was believed to be an immature form of more significant metals like gold, both physically and spiritually. Alchemists believed that metals were not unique elements, but were substances in different developmental stages on a journey to spiritual perfection. While the science of alchemy was never proven, it did set the stage for modern chemistry.

Church of Wicca

The School and Church of Wicca was founded in 1968 by Yvonne and Gavin Frost. It was the first Wiccan church to be federally recognized in the United States. It is best known for its academic correspondence related to the unique interpretations of Wicca by the Frosts. The School and Church reside in Beckley, West Virginia (Grimassi, 2000). Thousands and thousands of students started the School of Wicca's 12-lesson course, but the course is rigorous and only a few thousand have completed it (Guiley, 2008). It is believed that the Church of Wicca is responsible for starting at least one hundred covens.

The Church of Wicca believes in monotheism; there is only one God. The founders of the Church hold the point of view that God is unknowable, abstract, and without need to be worshiped. This is the primary difference from other traditions of Wicca. Also, unlike most Wiccan covens, there is no focus on the feminine or female deities. The Frosts believed that there are idols and stone gods that humans create to store energy, which can then be used for magical workings. The Wiccan Church taught "Sidhe," the astral realm. It also taught that each individual's spirit travels through a reincarnation system where it can learn. They also believed that the world's overpopulation was due to "inferior spirits" taking human form on earth (Doyle, 2016).

The Church held instruction on the practice of kundalini sex, including "introitus," in which sexual activities without reaching a climax or orgasm were performed as an expression of surrender to God. The School of Wicca's curriculum offered a variety of classes about the Wiccan religion, metaphysical practices, and the occult. Interestingly, the first class is titled Essential Witchcraft, which takes "a year and a day" to complete. The school curriculum also contains courses on Psychic and Herbal Healing, Practical Sorcery, Astral Projection, Advanced Shamanism and Celtic Witchcraft, Prediction, Spiritual Awareness, Astrology, and many more topics.

Finding the Right Coven

Covens usually have up to 13 members, but are often smaller. Larger covens take a chance on finding it hard to keep the group dynamics healthy. There are no rules set in stone in Wicca, there is no one single guidebook, and no governing or ruling bodies. Each coven functions uniquely according to its members' and leaders' will. It is bound by an oath of secrecy, both to tradition and to members. Covens hold their meetings secretly in a location where they practice magic and rituals. How often they get together varies, but usually they do celebrate Sabbats (the Wheel of the Year) and Esbats (full moons).

It is essential for your journey that you find the right coven that is a good fit for you; no two are the same. Some practice Wicca with influence of different traditions, such as the faerie tradition or the northern tradition, so it is worth it to do your homework before asking to join a specific coven. It is kind of like buying a new car, don't jump on the first one you see. Seasoned groups usually tell you to shop around before committing to their membership.

Remember, Wicca is a religion that never proselytizes. They don't actively try to recruit new members. When joining a coven, you will most likely be asked to demonstrate a level of commitment. You should show that you are sure this is the only spiritual life you want to live. The initiation oath includes living a life of service and a willingness to make the craft a priority. Many Wiccans and pagans are secretive (still in the broom closet), so most covens don't advertise their locations or provide overt information. So, networking is important. You may want to start the "seeking" process, which means letting it be known you are looking to join a coven. After the word of you being a seeker spreads, you may be approached by a local coven.

There are also Wiccan and Pagan websites for networking, such as Meetup Groups or Witchvox.com, but make sure you practice normal online safety precautions, the same as you would when meet any strangers. I always say, "Check it out." First, find, locate, and learn about your local Wiccan or Pagan community. While it is not always obvious right off the bat, most areas have Pagan communities. Most Pagan communities have a public facing aspect, as do Wiccan communities, so look for your tribe or coven providing classes or discussions (gatherings). Check out Pagan book shops where they also generally have a noticeboard that lets you know the where and when of the local chapters. Once you go to some of the gatherings, you will begin to meet members of the Wiccan or Pagan communities in a more social setting. Finding your coven is kind of like any other relationship. It is best done over time and gradually. Do not rush. Remember, this group includes people that you will be sharing your most vulnerable self with and the highs and the lows in your life. You want to be comfortable and feel safe sharing your secrets. They need to feel the same about you.

Steps for Starting a Coven

1. Consider your main goals. How many members do you want in your coven? Do you know who your possible candidates are? What do you want to achieve? Will there be complete equality or a hierarchy? Sit down and journal all the questions you can come up with about your new coven, put them down for a week, and then go back and answer them.
2. Put together your coven's grimoire, after you have answered all of your questions. Seek out possible members for your coven and start planning your first get together.
3. Remember not to pressure anyone to join just because you are excited. They may wish to stay solitary witches or may already belong to an exclusive coven. Either way, respect their decision.
4. At your first gathering talk about the new ideas you have for the coven. Maybe you want some type of attire or uniform for your meetings and rituals? Maybe you want to collaborate with your new members on an apothecary. The possibilities are endless!
5. Don't push people too far. If someone doesn't want to do something or they feel uncomfortable, forcing them to do something

can give you a bad reputation. Give respect and you will receive it.
6. Due to the fact that society, still to this day, doesn't support Wicca (although things are starting to change), think about the importance of starting a secret coven.
7. Put together your materials, such as herbs, crystals, candles, and essential oils. Smudge bundles are always good to donate to a group. They are good to keep around in case someone forgets an item needed for spell casting or ritual work.
8. Make a coven calendar! Decide which Esbats and Sabbats you are going to celebrate as a coven. Write some rituals and spells together with your new coven members. Maybe you'll have a wonderful kitchen witch to whip up some blessed food for the celebration or have a potluck.
9. To help increase the power of your coven, study new types of magic and spiritual arts, so you and your coven can uncover even more mysteries. Find and read books of shadows and spell crafting books together. Dig deeper into learning your brand of magic. Avoid dogmatism and keep an open mind.

Coven (the Wheel of the Year)

The Wheel of the Year is a religious celebration that occurs on each of the eight neo-pagan holidays. The Sabbats of the year include four festivals celebrating the changing seasons. The four solar festivals are: the fall equinox, summer solstice, spring equinox, and the winter solstice. The ancient Celts believed time was cyclical; people are born and die, seasons change, but all will again return in some aspect or another and the cycle repeats itself, naturally. Modern-day Wiccans celebrate the Wheel of the Year in remembrance of the importance of balance in an uncertain world. Jacob Grimm, an academic mythologist, coined the modern-day Wheel of the Year in 1835. By the 1950s it became solidified in the Wicca movement.

Wiccan Wheel of the Year Festivals

Name	Holiday	Earth Event	Date	Occasion
Samhain	Halloween	Fifteen Scorpio	October 31st	Cleaning and releasing. Celebrating the dead.
Yule	Christmas	Winter Solstice Capricorn	December 20-25	Song, fellowship, candlelight, and lighting the sacred fire.
Imbolc	Candlemas	Midway between the Winter Solstice and the Spring Equinox: Aquarius	February 1-2	Lunar Fire Festivals, day of feast and celebration for the recovery of the Earth Goddess after giving birth.
Ostara	Easter	Spring Equinox Aries	March 20-23	Spring cleaning; planting seeds.
Beltane	May Day	Taurus	April 30-May 1	Fertility; Fire celebration. Couples dancing around the fire.
Litha	Midsummer	Summer Solstice Gemini	June 20-22	Gratitude for light and life. Honors the Sun God.
Lughnasadh	First Harvest	Halfway between the summer solstice and autumn equinox Leo	August 1	Symbolic gifts of the first fruits given to priests as an offering to deity. Honoring hard work and that pays off.
Mabon	Thanksgiving	Autumnal	September	Time for resting

		equinox Virgo	20-23	after the hard work of the harvest. A time to reap what was sown. Time to finish up projects.

The eight Wiccan festivals are produced to bring awareness to all that has been gained or lost throughout the year. Ancient societies, such as the Celts, held the belief that a lack of gratitude was a sin that will take the sinner into a dark place, where bitterness, resentment, and self-pity live. In order to find balance in the world or in our lives, it is necessary to stop and reflect on those things we cherish and are grateful for.

Samhain: Halloween

Samhain denotes the beginning of the yearly cycle. It marks the end of the season of light or summer and the start of the season of darkness. Darkness is not associated with negativity to those who are Wiccan. It doesn't mean evil or sadness, as there cannot be light without dark. It is merely part of the human condition. Thanks for the past year are put forth during the Samhain celebrations and Wiccans reflect on the wonderful times they share with those who recently passed on to the other side. Samhain celebration and rituals are very much like the modern-day Halloween festivities held in the United States. Samhain is a recognition of the "in-between" time, where the spirits of the dead can move into the realm of the living more easily. It is a Wiccan tradition to leave out snacks or to prepare a feast to leave out for those spirits visiting from the other realms.

Witches who in the past have done something wrong to someone who has passed over don't wear Halloween masks, so the spirits of those they have wronged will recognize them when they come back seeking requital. However, wearing a disguise or mask during Samhain is customary, in an effort to ward off those fairies, spirits, and dead souls with the strongest powers that move at night to seduce or abduct mortals. Mischievous activities, such as bonfires, are also traditional for Samhain. Pagans believe that the world started in chaos and that the Goddesses and other forces of the divine created balance and order. This is why Halloween pranks are done to represent this chaos. The returning back to "normal" the following day symbolizes the restoration of order. Also, bonfires are lit to symbolize light amongst the darkness. This is a beautiful tradition.

Yule: Christmas

The winter solstice is celebrated as Yule when days start to become longer again. The winter solstice was seen by the ancient pagans as the birth of a new sun god of the year. Trees were traditionally believed to be sacred because they are home to deities and spirits. Very much like in Christmas traditions, an outdoor tree was decorated; in honor of the sun god's birthday, gifts were exchanged. Along with decorating a tree, bonfires were lit to symbolize the rebirth of light and new beginnings. People danced around the ignited Yule log, singing songs and tossing pieces of holly into the fire to represent the challenges of the past year. A piece of the Yule Log was kept for the next year's bonfire to symbolize continuity.

Also symbolized by Yule was the Oak King's victory over his brother, the Holly King. The entities of the two brothers represent the changing of the seasons. The earth is governed by the Oak King after his defeat of the Holly King in the winter, and he continues his reign until the coming of mid-summer or the Summer Solstice, when the Holly King retakes the battle, beating the Oak King. He then stays dominant during Yule. Wicca tradition is that the Oak King and the Holly King represent twin characteristics of the Horned God, with each one ruling half of the year. The battles are carried out to win the Goddess' favor, with the loser of the battle retreating to tend to his wounds for the other half of the year until he again returns to rule the Earth.

Imbolc: Candlemas

Imbolc takes place at the middle point between the Winter Solstice and the Spring Equinox, and corresponds with hope, pregnancy, purification, and fertility. In Old Irish, Imbolc means "in the belly of a pregnant sheep." The Imbolc festival represents a bright future, where dolls are weaved from wheat and corn stalks to pay tribute to Brigid, the Celtic goddess, and to symbolize continuity, good luck, and fertility. The fertility goddess, Brigid, is celebrated in early spring and marked in the United States by Groundhog Day.

Ostara: Easter

Ostara follows Imbolc and pays tribute to the Spring Equinox. Ostara celebrations mirror Easter festivities, including dying eggs, baby chicks, fancy feasts, and rabbits. The meaning of the word Ostara is rooted in the German lore as the fertility goddess and springtime. Eostre means mother of the dawn and in Wiccan tradition, she comes back from under the earth where she slept for the months leading up to her pregnancy with the next sun god to be born on each Yule.

Rebirth and renewal are emphasized on Ostara, which pays tribute to the importance of the egg symbolism. The notion of the labyrinth is also prominent. The labyrinth goes back to the Neolithic Age over 12,000 years ago, in areas as diverse as Ireland, India, and Greece. Ostara represents that aspect of yourself where you separate your personal external reality in search of a greater meaning unique to yourself. The traditional Easter Egg hunt is a portrayal of the search for heightened awareness.

Beltane: May Day

Beltane marks the coming of summer when bonfires burn freely in traditional Wiccan fashion. The bonfires of Beltane symbolize passion and the disinhibition of oneself to indulge in one's desires. The word "Beltane" means "bright fire" and represents fertility and light. Dancing is a common activity at a Beltane festival and circling a tree was common in ancient times. In modern days, people dance around a Maypole, which is a phallic symbol decorated with long strands of ribbon which are held by dancers as they circle around. Mayday is celebrated all over Europe and corresponds with Beltane. As dark days start to become increasingly light, all of nature awakens, including fairies, spirits, and other celestial entities. Pagans routinely enact cleansing rituals to protect themselves from mischievous fairy spells. They take lighted candles to each corner of the home, from side to side and front to back, connecting eight points that set an invisible protective shield that manifests harmony and balance.

Litha: Midsummer/Summer Solstice

Litha celebrates the longest day of the year, the Summer Solstice. The Holly King defeats his twin brother, the Oak King, on this day in June, and the days grow shorter. The festival of Litha is celebrated with a feast of honey cakes, fresh fruits, dancing, and bonfires. It is the commemoration of light overcoming the darkness with the knowledge that, in the future, the darkness will once again reign over the light. This signifies the temporary nature of longer nights and shorter days. Some people take marriage vows on Litha, as part of the festival. Sun wheels are constructed from wheat and corn stalks, and protection rituals are performed. Wiccans are very creative with their ritual plans on Litha. Water is blessed by magic to manifest abundance in their gardens and prosperity spells are cast under the midsummer's night sky. Litha inspires inner power and brightness in all witches; small fires burn in the pots of one's home and the magic of love is in the air.

Lughnasadh: First Harvest

Lughnasadh marks the change of season from summer to autumn, and it is celebrated with a harvest festival. The first fruits of the harvest are ceremoniously offered to the gods and goddesses. Lugh was the god of light in early Irish lore. His mother, Tailtiu, succumbed to the hard work of plowing and land preparation. Lughnasadh is in honor of Lugh's mother's sacrifice; each year a funeral feast is held. Modern day pagans sport competitions in fencing, foot racing, horse-racing, and archery. It is also the last celebration before summer's end.

Mabon: Thanksgiving

Named in 1097, Mabon celebrates thoughts and Thanksgiving for all that has been gained and lost over the last year. It is the Autumn Equinox festival, named after the Welsh God, son of the Earth Mother Goddess, and symbolizes the second harvest. Wiccans and pagans alike bring seasonal gatherings, such as apples and grapes, and place them upon an altar, as they prepare a feast for family and friends.

Apples are a common symbol of the second harvest and rituals give way in thanks to the gods and goddesses for the bountiful harvest of Mabon, as well as celebrating a day of equal light. On Mabon, night and day have an equal length. They are in perfect harmony once again. Feminine and masculine, light and dark, and inner and outer are perfectly balanced, but Mabon holds the cusp of change as the darkness begins to creep back upon the light of day. The days will grow shorter and begin to cool. The sap in the trees will return to their roots, and the green of the summer will again be transformed into wondrous oranges, golds, yellows, and the other fiery colors of fall, returning all to the darkness from whence we came.

Mabon is a time to give thanks for the Sun's diminishing light and for all the bounties provided. Each turn of the Wheel brings outer and inner gifts, insights, and a time for rest after the labor of the harvest. It is a time to finish our projects, clear out any clutter of what we no longer need or want, and prepare for the descent into winter. As we do this, we need to be looking forward to new hopes and aspirations and new ideas that will flourish in the dark, eagerly waiting for spring to return.

Hermetic Order of the Golden Dawn

The Hermetic Order of the Golden Dawn of the late 19th century was a magical order that practiced various types of spells and spiritualism. Magic and ritual concerts become the center stone of Wiccan and many other traditions. Much of today's spiritual magic was taken from the Golden Dawn tradition (Llewellyn Encyclopedia, 2008). Much like Masonic lodges, the Golden Dawn system was based on initiation and hierarchy. There are three Orders, with the "Golden Dawn" being the first; however, oftentimes, all three Orders are referred to as the "Golden Dawn."

The Golden Dawn Order provided teaching about the philosophy of the occult or esotericism, and was grounded in personal development and the Hermetic Qabalah through awareness and the study of the tarot, divination, astrology, geomancy, and the four classical elements. The Inner Order or the Second Order provided the teachings of magic, including astral projection, scrying, and alchemy; it was also called the Order of Rose of Ruby and Cross of Gold (Rosae Rubeae et Aureae Crucis). The Chiefs of Third Order of the Secret were said to be highly skilled spiritual communicators who directed the lower two order's activities.

Choosing a God or Goddess

To have a healthy relationship with a God or Goddess, you need to establish a relationship. Like most relationships, you don't start one out of need, nor do you pick one out like you're choosing a handbag color. You do not have to believe in or worship a god or goddess to be a witch, and you don't have to pray to a specific God or Goddess to be a Pagan. However, it may be part of your spiritual practices to form some type of relationship with a named Goddess or God but remember, in ancient history, most of the Goddesses and Gods were worshiped, and they usually had high priests who performed most of the work.

How to Choose a Matron or Patron Deity

In most Pagan and witchcraft religions, Goddesses and Gods are frequently used terms. Some religions center their focus on gender duality, and some focus on just one God. You can believe in a single Goddess or many, but Wiccan spend most of their time invested in Matron and Patron deities. You don't have to necessarily refer to them as Patron or Matron, some deities don't actually like the whole idea of being your Matron or Patron because they're not quite up to playing a parental role in your life. Some would much rather function as a well-respected peer or even Moon Goddess or Supreme Goddess. They are individualistic and they each desire something different from each one of us.

Most pagans worship some type of main deity or a few main deities, but it isn't necessarily a parental (fatherly or motherly) type of a relationship. The exact type of relationship you will have with your deities depends on both you and the deity involved. No two people worship the same way. You can start with books and the internet. When you find a spirit whose qualities you like, give them some time and a few offerings over a period of a month or so. Ask them for a sign that they hear you. You may receive an animal sighting, a recurring number, a song, or you may feel their impact directly on some area of your life that suddenly improves. Once contact is established, invoke them in your spell crafting, starting with something small, or send them a prayer. Always remain sure that your initial requests sit firmly in the deity's wheelhouse. Journal your results. Did you enjoy their energy? Was your request fulfilled? If your results were positive, continue to offer thanks and provide offerings, always asking for signs and opening your mind to seeing them.

You can target a deity based upon your life circumstances, local spirits, or a specific deity you would like to honor. You can use a search engine to come up with links, books, and pages about every specific deity from any specific Pantheon. Look into the Elements and Spirits, Gods and Goddesses of healing, justice, culinary works, or anything else.

However, these should just be jumping off points to your in-depth research.

Other types of documents:

- Legends and myths
- Archaeological and historical evidence and books.
- Poems and hymns
- Texts written by reconstructionists.

Worshipping and Working with a Deity

Not all Goddesses and Gods are the same, so it's essential to your spiritual life to get to know the ones you want to work with. The idea of the appropriate or right way to worship and give offerings should be in a way that is conducive to the needs or demands of the Goddess or God in question. Get to know the legends and myths related to the respected group they are associated with and study these stories. For instance, if you are devoted to the Greek Goddesses and Gods, read the Homeric writings and hymns. If your path is Celtic, go over the *Mabinogion*, and reach out and ask them to flat-out tell you what they need.

Put some thoughts into how you honor the Goddesses and Gods. Ask yourself what you want to achieve by making the offering. Maybe you are just expressing your gratitude or maybe you have a specific request. The most important thing to do when trying to worship or work with a deity is to study those divine beings of your tradition, so that when you conduct a ritual in their name or give an offering, you can do it in a way that truly honors them.

Chapter Two:

How to Learn Magic in the Modern World

Magic is used every day by millions in the modern world, whether you believe it or not! Modern day society puts great effort into controlling people's perceptions and thoughts about the everyday world. Agenda setting theory is a social engineering technique that aims to vastly shift our perception and used to be called psychological warfare. Magic is a way to take your power back and control the events in your life, rather than being a victim of mass media's brainwashing.

What is Magic and How It Can Help You?

Magic is a personal journey in which you learn how to use your senses to navigate this world. Modern magic is often defined as accomplishing the impossible. The accepted definition of magic is utilizing perception to interact with and influence the world. We shouldn't think of it as "doing the impossible," because that pushes magic into fantasy rather than a method for improving the quality of our lives. Over the last thousand years, religion and science have shoved magic to the outer edges of perception and essentially taken it out of the hands of people. Science and religion seem to have claimed the exclusive right to shape how people perceive the world. Nowadays, society leaves people with little choice about what faith is and then punishes those who have the courage to look at the world differently. Because of this, society's development is skewed. The world needs magic. We need to have the ability to perceive all of the options life has to offer and allow us to function as explorers in life.

For many individuals, magic is just another way of connecting with your potential. You use your perception and intuition to explore your available potential and then pick an action to tap into that potential. It isn't uniquely special as some may think, as is the case when any real-life event gets compared to movies. Working with your potential is a way to help you connect to what is hidden to your normal senses and what is in plain sight. Part of magic is learning how to carefully listen to the silence.

Collecting Magical Energy

There are many different types of magical energy. Let's divide it into three magical categories: spiritual, mental, and physical. Most people's perceptions revolve around the physical world, so this is where the average person sees magic. There are also many magic styles:

1. Transformation or alteration: Rearranging the definition of something.
2. Evocation or conjuration: Becoming aware of something new.
3. Divination: Gathering new information and exploring new insights.

Spirits are real, but they don't directly manifest into the physical world. Just because something is real, doesn't make it a physical reality. Society is a real entity but not a physical one, it exists only in our minds. Society is a manifestation of people who then construct physical artifacts. Certain physical manifestations of society act as reinforcements for a society that is consumer-based.

Spirits are representations of reality; they are not of the physical world. When we experience something spiritual, it is a description of an experience which is outside of the physical. After the spiritual experience is complete, the individual is left with a memory which is then understood as a mind-based experience. Unfortunately, the media and wishful thinking encourages us to magnify our spiritual experiences, much like those tales told about the size of the fish you caught that expand over time. So, spiritual magic is very real, but tends to be much more subtle that one might think and not nearly as flashy.

We are a microcosm and a macrocosm; we are each an individual, while at the same time, we are the universe. Magic based in the spiritual realm is subtle. Since spirit is independent of the physical world, using spirit (real magic) is much like constructing a sandcastle, a temporary structure. It is not attempting to attach itself to reality, yet it does impact the world and then it gently washes away. As you continue to see and learn magic, remember it is subtle, not long lasting. But what is everlasting? Even the vastness of the mountains, with time, erodes to sand. Just as a firefly will only dance for an evening, the magical experience can last in the form of a story.

Magic and Modernity

As the exploration of spirituality outside of the boundaries of traditional religion continues to grow, ritual and spell crafting and magical ways of healing are now attracting the interest of the masses. What is quickly becoming an acceptable form of spiritualism was once banished to the outer fringes of society.

Meditation, tarot, and astrology and other beginner-level concepts have given way to an interest in astral projection, aura cleansing, reiki, spell-crafting, moon worshipping, and dream reading for many people.

Modern life can be very chaotic and it's perfectly crafted to take us away from being present. Rituals are a practice in mindfulness. Tea ceremonies and meditation are ancient methods of grounding. People are looking for a more spiritual and sacred way of life. We are all seeking a deep connection with other people, plants and animals, the elements, and ourselves. We want to be one with nature again, rather than sticking out like a sore thumb. We need that balance in order to help us during these trying times.

Bringing Technology into Magic

Advanced, ever-present magic almost always seems to work the same as technology. Car engines are powered by the element fire, but we don't think about it like that, we just get in and drive away. We don't need to acquire special talents to use our phones, as they appear to work like magic. There's even a new word, "Magitech!" A combination of modern technology and magic. Magic and technology have science in common, in that they are things to be learned, studied, and experimented with.

Living in this modern digital age can have serious mental health consequences. Social media and the ability of others to reach us 24/7 provide people with more opportunities to access our auric fields and our energy supply. Don't worry though, magic comes to the rescue. We can use your magical tools for protection in the technological realm, just like we do for protection in other realms. It is like having a protection spell for your cell.

Enacting magic that impacts the technological realm, or technomancy, improves the way machines work, can elevate our status on social media, and can help to ward off negative confrontations with others online (Stardust, 2021). We should perform technomancy at least every other day. Here are some tips on how to perform technomancy:

1. Smudge your phone with *palo santo* or *sage* to release static energy. Our cell phones are like a gateway to the world. This is why it is so important to cleanse the energy we receive and give. This can help to make sure we are receiving positive and constructive information, not the type that causes distress or blurs our judgement.
2. Keep a *shungite* or *black tourmaline* crystal near your phone. Shungite is a healing and purifying stone, so it is perfect for mending

anyone you may have argued with. It also helps you dissociate your energy from those psychic leeches who won't stop calling you. Black tourmaline cleanses our devices and removes unwanted or negative energy. Crystals are excellent detoxifying agents and will help you to gain better privacy, while at the same time boosting your likes on social media because they draw positive energy and people are drawn to positivity.

3. Envision sacred geometry. Picturing sigils or pentagrams or other powerful symbols project divine protection. Just like in other areas of life, projection magic makes sure we don't receive hateful drama in our electromagnetic realm, and only allows positive energies to enter into our smart devices.

4. Keep your mantras close by. Have a mantra on hand to help you if you find yourself arguing, gossiping, or experiencing any other type of negativity in a conversation. "Delete, cancel, block, clear" is one affirmation that will bounce gloomy sentiments off of your auric field, so it doesn't influence your positive vibrations.

5. Keep your mindset golden. Imagine a golden glow around your computer or phone. It will

ward off haters and pull in more positive people.

Finding Your Magic Place

It seems obvious to trust your intuition, however, like everything in life, refining your intuition takes practice and skill. Throughout the day, we are confronted with pressure, suggestions, and opinions from the outside world; what is right and what is wrong, and what we shouldn't or should do. During our development, the challenges we face are supposed to build our confidence and self-esteem; however, that doesn't always happen and instead we stuff our inner voice deep within us to accept someone else's views. To find your way, you need to know who you are, you have to know your beliefs, and what makes you happy and what makes you sad. Learning how to use your intuition or your inner compass can help you do those things. When you're faced with a problem or a choice, the first place you should seek an answer is within, so the advice you get is from someone you can trust.

First, you should be learning how your intuition works. Is it a slight grumbling in the back of your mind or a word or image in your head? A feeling you should turn right instead of left? Acquiring the skill of identifying how your intuition presents itself and the difference from feeling like a passing thought will help you to practice ways in which you can pay attention to how and when your intuition manifests. It can also present itself in shadow work, in your dreams, via tarot, or during a nature walk.

Witches have learned how to finely tune their intuition, but newer witches have to learn how to trust it. One way to learn how to listen to your intuition is to stop thoughts that try to interfere with it. For instance, you are on a shopping trip and you suddenly get a thought that you left the oven on. Immediately afterward you get another thought that discredits your intuition and tells you that you worry too much. There are many ways we have been conditioned to not pay attention to our intuition. Pay attention to yourself, don't ignore that voice. Listen to learn and learn to listen! Maybe you get an uneasy feeling about traveling on some road that you normally take or an uneasy feeling about purchasing something online. It is not really about if it comes true, it is about taking every opportunity to practice listening and learning how to decipher what your intuition is trying to tell you through experimentation. As you learn and practice listening to yourself, your intuition will become stronger, and you will be able to rely on it more. Try wearing some pearl or moonstone crystals to sharpen your intuition and learn how to listen.

Frank's Boost Your Intuition Spell

Materials:

- Pearl or moonstone crystal
- Silver coin
- Clear quartz crystal
- Rosemary
- Lemongrass oil
- A blue candle

Instructions

1. Smudge the area and sit in a comfortable position.
2. Anoint your blue candle with the lemongrass oil.
3. Light the candle.
4. Place the moonstone or pearl crystal in one hand and the clear quartz in the other hand and place your hands in your lap.
5. Place the coin between you and the candle, creating a symbolic bridge of elements from the flame to your body.
6. Close your eyes, center yourself, and chant:

    Grant me the intuition
    That I may know my truth
    With moonstone in my hand
    And pearls of wisdom from the sand
    Let chaos be gone
    With the silver of the dawn

Make me bright like the snow
From within I will know
So mote it be

Daily Passive Magic

Meditation is one of the daily passive magical practices of Wicca. In order to manifest effective magic, you need to acquire the skill of entering a place within you that is calm and deeply relaxed to align and balance yourself with the natural energies and forces around you. As you learn to be still and quiet your mind and enter into a deep state of calmness, you will learn how to become centered, focused, and balanced; you are learning how to mentally discipline yourself. It is in this place in your inner being that you will join together with your spirit self and your guide through the path you have chosen to take. You can use your magical tools to help you on your journey, such as candles, incense, music, singing, chanting, drumming, and guided imagery to put your mind into a meditative state.

Once you learn how to listen to your spirit and trust yourself, options begin to appear. Things that seemed vague or impossibly subtle begin to become clear and attainable in your awareness because you have a better understanding of yourself. You can visualize your near future and the choices you are about to make that may be wrong or right. Many things will come to you while in this state that projects you into the space between the material and celestial.

Another daily passive magical activity is a simple walk in the park or somewhere in nature. It has the astonishing power to enhance your well-being, realign your spiritual awareness, and broaden your knowledge as a witch. Wild crafting is one way to get in touch with your daily magical practices. Instead of buying a $55 wreath from Walmart or a craft shop, take a walk, find some beautiful evergreens, and create something wonderful with the magic of a tree. Take a course on wild edibles and then look for a few while on your walk. Cooking with lavender, wild onions, and wild berries puts the magic of plants right in your tummy. Check out the tiniest details while on your magical nature walk. Look at the tiny flowers, and the veins running through the leaves, and the penny-sized mushrooms you came close to stepping on. These are magical things. The geometric magic of a honeycomb and the sweeping, broad landscapes will leave you with a wild sense of wonder.

There are endless ways to practice daily passive magic; even when it comes to your evening showers, there is magic to be had. Spiritual bathing has more intent than just cleaning off and it has been used traditionally in every culture, often to cleanse the soul, heal your chakras, and heal your spirit. Spiritual bathing clears blockages that can often lead to more serious problems. You have to make your tub a sacred space. That means no clutter and a spic-n-span tub. You add the magic in the form of oils, herbs, flowers, and most of all intention. You need to focus on spiritual healing, so that means unplugging all of your smart devices.

Speaking to the Nature of Spells

Nature plays a huge role in the Wiccan culture and magic. One of the ways we speak to the nature of spells is by physically connecting with the elements, starting with the earth. Earthing is the spiritual process of experiencing magic by physically connecting with the earth. Touching the earth brings together the spiritual and the physical. Studies have indicated that skin to earth contact has a significant effect on our wellness, both physically and emotionally (Oschman et al., 2015). The body's stress hormones are reduced, blood pressure is lowered, heart rate decreases, and an overall calming effect results from earthing or skin-to-earth contact (Chevalier et al., 2019). Connecting to the earth this way may also introduce you to the local spirits wishing to start a relationship with you!

Many pagans, wiccans, pantheists, and New Agers, practice nature religion, the oldest magic spell of them all. As previously discussed, variants of animism and a belief in the forces of nature, as well as a belief in the spiritual realms, are common themes to most nature religions. Even those adhering to scientism and atheism, who hold the belief that nature does not hold magic, still accept the fact that it has the ability to generate feelings of wonder, mystery, and awe, all of which are mystical. Many Wiccans and pagans are focused on green magic and the concept that deities and other powers of the supernatural realms can be recognized through directly experiencing natural objects and natural events. Monotheism is part nature religion and many people believe that nature as one entity is sacred and even divine. There are no scriptures, prophets, and holy books in this religion. However, it does serve society through focusing on our connection with nature.

In the spirit of the nature religion, all things of the universe (not created by humans) are collective and bonded by a labyrinthine web of life force or energy, including humans. All members are considered clergy, with both women and men found in leadership positions for ritual events, but only temporarily. There are no permanent hierarchical relationships established in nature religion. There are no buildings erected for gatherings. Sacred spaces for ritual are in the natural environment, not in brick-and-mortar establishments. This is not to say that members of nature religion do not have get-togethers in someone's home, because gatherings to plan religious activities in nature can be structured in such a way.

Controlling Your Energy

Energy is a tangible, moving life force that is easily understandable in the context of our day-to-day feelings (lethargic and sluggish or the opposite, invincible). Usually we blame our days of low energy on unhealthy food or a lack of a good night's sleep. It is, however, much more complex than that. We can have a conscious relationship with our energy system. Sometimes, we really complicate the concept of energy by trying to define it in mystical or scientific terms. To really understand what it is, all you have to do is be still and feel into your surroundings and yourself. For instance, when we are crying or laughing, we may feel a release of energy. When feeling calm, we're grounded.

Certain people or circumstances can drain our energy. Also, sometimes when we are in situations in life where we feel less than ideal, we may lean on others using their energy as our own fuel source. Even our personal boundaries are a source of energy. We can let our energy openly flow when we want to share with others, or tighten it up when we want to detach. One of the things we learned in elementary science class is that energy cannot be destroyed but it can be altered. When depleted of energy, a system can collapse. Despite the strength of its power, energy on its own is neutral. It is our consciousness that decides its direction and movement. If we comprehend what it means to be conscious of our energy, we can better direct our energy toward connection, evolution, and creation. The less we comprehend how to be conscious of our energy, the more stagnant, separated, and even self-destructive we become.

I learned a great deal about how to restore my energetic integrity and what it means for my energy systems to be blocked. All of us know what it feels like to be open and flexible. When our energy is flowing freely, we breathe easier and have an overall sense of spaciousness. When our energy flow is balanced, our mind, body, and spirit work with each other in partnership. We trust ourselves and the process. This is called energetic integrity. Many of us feel that energetic integrity is temporary. Sometimes, it seems blocked, stuck, or stagnant. Our thinking becomes narrower and more fixed. We breathe unevenly, sometimes holding our breath, and feel our muscles begin to tighten or weaken. There is a general feeling of being ungrounded or detached from our power. Sometimes, it feels like we lose our footing, which is a feeling of being unbalanced and only able to act submissively or aggressively.

We often tend to block out our personal energy to avoid unwanted impulses or feelings. Very similar to repressing our emotions, this is a defense mechanism that allows us to block unwanted thoughts or emotions. For instance, think about a school age child. Every day, the child goes to school and runs up to her teacher proudly handing in her homework on time. Each time she does this, her teacher places the homework in a pile, and instructs the child to take her seat. The child senses this as a form of rejection, and begins to restrict her feelings of excitement and her impulse to run up to her teacher. She starts to tell herself a story so she can make sense of her experience. Over time, repressing her emotions will begin to contract her energy flow. When the little girl grows up, we may see an adult who struggles with expressing her feelings and may have physically distant relationships. Her life may have the main goal of avoiding humiliation and rejection and the associated pain that accompanies it at all costs.

It takes a bit of self-exploration to learn how to restore your energetic integrity. It takes willingness, patience, and risk. It becomes a task of learning how to become increasingly conscious of your energy flow and to learn how to use your energy to stay separate or to defend. It is about getting in touch with your belief systems and notice where you distort reality as a means of adapting. With time, you can start to see the different methods you use your energy to defend yourself against certain emotions and experiences. Only then can you appreciate how manipulating your energy in this way blocks you from reaching your full potential that comes with embracing your energy as a full life force.

At first, I thought this was an avenue for personal growth, then I began to understand the relationship between my consciousness and my own energy. That translated into understanding the connection between consciousness and energy in systems as a whole within which we live. This applies to politics, our family life, the way we interact with the environment, finances, and even war. For instance, what if monetary wealth is just a cognitive distortion regarding safety? When we lack the consciousness of our energy flow, distortions can be found just about everywhere in ourselves and in society. If we start the work of transforming distorted energy back into its natural flow, we will be able to effect actual change in both society and in ourselves.

Steps for how to get to know you own energy system:

1. Thoughts are energy forms, so start to generate an awareness of your thinking. Start with the first thought you have upon waking and take it from there. Notice how and when your thoughts are flexible (how things can be) or fixed (how they are).
2. Several times per day, pause and close your eyes. Travel inward and check on if you feel present, how you are breathing, if you are relaxed or tense, tired or rested.
3. Take the time to move different parts of your body and notice if any feelings or thoughts arise. Are there some parts of your body that create emotions when energized by movement? Roll your head across your shoulders and note your feelings.
4. Make vocal sounds, either alone or with other people. Energize your "no" and "yes." Is one easier to say than the other? Are you even willing to make a sound?
5. Ask yourself where the energy currents are in your life. Are you emotionally fatigued by the demands of others or are you forcing your energy onto other people or situations?
6. Notice the changes in your energy levels when in the presence of different people. Does

your breathing change? Do your muscles contract?
7. Get together with a friend and play around with your energetic boundaries. Stand in front of each other and slowly walk towards each other and check out when you start to feel their energy. Does their energy make you feel less grounded? Can you use your voice to ask them to back away or to come closer? Feel the energy.
8. Journal your feelings according to your beliefs, and write down where in your body you feel these feelings if you feel them at all.
9. How do you approach the world? Do you lead with your hands, heart, or head?
10. Ask other people how they experience your energy.

Modern Magical Energy

Modern magic, like all things in life, can't operate without fuel. How far can you travel in your car without stopping for gas? How long can you go without a meal? Everything in the universe needs nourishment, including your spirit. Increasing your supply of energy to fuel your magic is a powerful way to enhance your spell work. If you want to practice real magic, you need real power, the type that doesn't run out and leave you spiritually stranded. There are many forms of modern magic activities you can use to raise your energy levels, such as dancing, chanting, drumming, forest bathing, and even sex. These are all powerful ways for enhancing your magical powers, but the real witch crafting comes from learning how to harness the power of the universe to manifest your desires, your destiny, and your sacred self. It takes a richer, deeper, and wider approach to energy work, one that moves you past your limitations and into spiritual enlightenment. Lifting up energy and projecting it to manifest your intent, is the modern way of working with energy to make magic or cast a spell. It is what happens when you learn how to really use your wand.

Remember, the universe is half feminine and half masculine and they both need each other for fertile and generative life processes to exist. The courtship and joining of the feminine and masculine are the energy that transforms, moves, and creates the universe. Likewise, while projecting energy is a powerful source of magic, the ability to receive it is just as powerful a tool. The following are six types of modern magical energy:

1. *Arcane Energy*: Glowing light is the most magical type of energy with an unknown origin. It is the energy of black magic, found

within spell books and magical items that bend the very fabric of reality to manifest intent and desire.
2. *Death Energy:* The energy produced from decay and death is naturally forming. Its color is dark purple, black, or putrid green and it occurs naturally in crypts, tombs, and things that have decayed for a very long time. This type of energy is used like grasping hands to drain its victims of their energy level.
3. *Aesthete Energy:* This corresponds with all things beautiful, such as aurora borealis, clouds, and vistas. This energy field forms around beautiful objects in nature or natural works of art. It can be manifested by those with artistic skills in music and poetry. This energy is not seen, yet travels like music and enhances everything it touches. Magic songs created by elves and fairies can lure people into a trance, or can be used to enchant a place or person with beauty.
4. *Glacial Energy:* This energy pertains to glaciers and ice and the unfeeling and unchanging cold. It can be found in icicles, glaciers, and other ancient frozen zones or it can even be the downy fur plucked from a newborn penguin.

5. *Verdant Energy:* This energy is the energy of nature and its color is bright green or dark red. It is a powerful energy that is overpowering and uncontrolled and is only found in the bellows of the most massive and ancient of trees. When conquered by a witch, it doesn't just make them more powerful or heal them, it also sharpens their senses to become equal to those of an animal. This type of energy is hardly ever used, except by Druids; even they are very careful and keep it at the end of a long wand or stick to avoid being contaminated.
6. *Interspatial Energy:* This energy is hidden in spaces within other spaces. It can be harvested carefully from complex architectures. Its color is clear or a dark orange glow. It gathers underneath things and in corners. When used as magic, it holds the keys to the realms within or interspatial realms. These realms are filled with symbols, creatures, and treasures of the inner spaces. When used carefully, it can unleash your hidden potential or even lessen the weight of one's soul.

Chapter Three:

Different Types of Witchcraft and Witches

There are various types of witches in the world today. For most witches, spell casting and magic are considered a skill set, and not always a form of religion. Therefore, people of any religion can practice magic no matter what their spiritual background is. There are also many types of witchcraft that are well-suited for all areas of our lives.

Modern Witchcraft

The meaning of modern witchcraft depends on who you ask. To most of us, a witch is the epitome of owning your own truth and all the power that comes with it. To wiccans, witches are religiously affiliated with the beliefs and traditions of Wicca. To some other witches, magic is part of their wellness regime or a manifestation of their creativity. Most modern witchcraft entails altar assemblies, spell work, and rituals. Modern witchcraft affords witches the opportunity to attend a fall-equinox ritual or sign up for magic-making classes. The use of candles, crystals, essential oils, and herbs in magic has become a very lucrative industry. Witches can be sought online to purchase spells made to fit your needs, and some witches are hired to cast spells on your behalf.

Genetic Witchcraft

As you come to know more individuals involved in Paganism, you will sometimes come across someone who claims to be a genetic witch or that they were born a witch. However, there is no such thing as "witch DNA." But there isn't Christian, Hindu, or Muslim DNA either. Being Wiccan usually means believing and doing things in such a way that makes you a witch. However, you can be raised in a Wiccan family, but that doesn't make you born Wiccan.

Some people are born with greater psychic abilities than others, and it may run in their family, but as far as identifying witch chromosomes, there is no such thing. However, I believe we all have psychic abilities and we just have to learn how to tap into them, rather than repressing them, as most people do. Oh, and by the way, people with Salem ancestry are not witches either. But certainly, there are hereditary witchcraft traditions; however, they are not inherited genetically. Some witchcraft traditions are passed down through generations and they tend to keep strong ties with the family of origin's witchcraft practices. For instance, some families follow Celtic gods, and practice a tradition of folk magic.

Kitchen Witchcraft

Using magic when preparing food for loved ones, is like adding some tender love and care (TLC) to each dish. TLC is the strongest magical ingredient used in kitchen witchcraft. Preparing meals with your own two hands and herbs from your windowsill infuses your dishes with magic. There is a sacredness in kitchen witchcraft that can change the way you imagine, prepare, and enjoy your meals. Kitchen witchcraft is spell work at its most basic level. The more you develop your magical repertoire, the more you will realize the wealth of magic that can be performed on a daily basis.

Kitchen witchcraft involves some wonderful magical tools, cauldrons, and candles. A stovetop altar creates an ambiance that is magically inspired. Keeping the kitchen as a sacred space is a very important component to kitchen witchery. There is no harmony in chaos and clutter. A book of shadows just for your kitchen will keep a tally of your culinary witchcraft.

Chanting while stirring, in either deosil (clockwise) or widdershins (counterclockwise) directions is like adding fairy dust to your recipe.

Humanities Witchcraft

There are federally recognized and well-respected Wiccan non-profit religious groups today. Their covens charge no dues or tithes. While Christian, Muslim, and Jewish churches qualify for grant monies to the tune of millions, pagans and Wiccans do not. However, humanitarian witchcraft does participate in the following activities:

- Activism: Spiritual and social programs, medical marijuana, peace, and others.
- Advocacy: On behalf of persecuted and abused pagans.
- Divination: Global efforts and hundreds of methods of divination.
- Education: Clergy training, interviews, lectures, mentions (in numerous books), tours, writing articles, books, and websites.
- Herbal: Resources, aid, guidance.
- Home: Acquisition, blessing, ghost-banishing, selling.
- Inmates: Nationwide Pagan advocacy.

- Legal: Aid, child custody cases, resources, unfair laws and policies elimination.
- Magical: Aid, guidance, teaching.
- Medical: Aid, guidance, resources.
- Military: Conscientious objector and base coven advocacy.
- Personal: Counseling.
- Rites: All rites of passage, elaborate/free public Sabbats, handfasting, legal marriages, rites for departed souls.

Criminal Witchcraft

Most have learned about the infamous Salem witchcraft trials, but there were many more. In some regions of the world, there are still laws prohibiting the practice of witchcraft. In the U.S. there are laws in some states making divinatory practices and fortune telling a criminal offense, to protect vulnerable citizens from the many swindles of con artists. Wiccans and pagans, alike, need to be familiar with their rights as an employee, parent, or active force military personnel. However, these are more along the lines of anti-fraud laws, not anti-witchcraft, and are usually part of zoning regulations.

There are reported cases in the U.S. in which certain witchcraft practices have been taken to court. This happened mostly in cases of animal sacrifice rituals that were deemed a public health concern and a violation of animal cruelty acts. Specifically, in New Orleans, this law burdens the free exercise of religious practices. However, this case was overturned, because there was not sufficient evidence in support of the health concern and the courts ruled in favor of the right to practice animal sacrifice. This is a hot topic for pagans and Wiccans, with valid arguments on both sides.

Wiccans and other earth-based practitioners have equal rights as do all other citizens of this country. Like everyone else, your legal rights against religious discrimination apply. Make sure you document each and every event if you are a victim of discrimination. Remember, if it's not documented, it didn't happen. Journal any events or conversations as they happen in real time. It is important to understand that opinions and discrimination are two different things. You are being religiously discriminated against if you are denied the same unalienable rights on the basis of your religion than other people.

Your rights as a Wiccan or pagan parent stand when your child attends a United States public school, the same as any other parents' rights. Keep in mind that most teachers have not had Wiccan or pagan students in their classroom before. With that said, here is an opportunity for setting a precedent for other pagan and Wiccan students. If your child comes home and tells you that their teacher said something unkind, don't rush off to the school board, go and talk to the teacher.

Let's say you have decided to come out of the broom closet, and you are facing getting fired from your job because of it, even though you have an excellent work history. In this case, you should seek the advice of a civil rights lawyer who specializes in Wiccan and Pagan discrimination cases. Remember to document every event.

If you or someone you care about are a member of the military, familiarize yourself with your rights as a Wiccan or Pagan soldier. First, go through the proper military channels, if you or a person you know suffers religious discrimination. If that doesn't work, contact the Inspector General (IG). They shoulder the responsibility for investigating these types of complaints. If you still do not experience positive results, you can file an Article 138 complaint (Wigington, 2020).

Grandmotherly Witchcraft

Many of us come from a long line of witches. Sometimes this knowledge is kept hidden until a child comes of age and can make their own decisions regarding witchcraft. But, if you are wondering if you come from a lineage of witches, here are ten telltale signs that your grandmother(s) may have been a witch:

1. *Elixirs and Potions*: Grandmotherly witchcraft usually has a potion for just about everything. It is the first turn-to when you feel under the weather. They can taste awful, but they do the trick.
    a. Castor oil is well known for its healing properties, and is referred to as 'palm of Christ or Palma Christi' in some cultures.
    b. Cinnamon
    c. Garlic
    d. Onion
    e. Honey
    f. Lemon
    g. Salt
    h. Corked-topped glass bottles containing tinctures.
    i. Pot liquor: the liquid leftover after making greens (kale or collard greens) and used as a tincture.
    j. Wheat germ
    k. Goldenseal
    l. Things pulled from the backyard
2. *Spirits:* Grandmotherly witchcraft is always chock full of spirits: nefarious spirits, friendly spirits, old spirits, and even spirits cloaked in

black. Grandmothers do not seem particularly worried and are usually accustomed to the spirits they live with, as well as the occasional visitors. They are rarely evil spirits; they just are who they are!

3. *Unflinching Grandmothers*: There is little that rattles or shakes grandmothers. This is just part of the natural outcome of them knowing who they are and their powers. One of my friend's grandma was sitting at a baseball game when a drunk spectator started falling down the bleachers right toward her. She didn't bat an eye. Suddenly, two teenage boys jumped in front of her and broke the man's fall. Not a hair on her body was touched. She never flinched.

4. *Hair:* Grandmotherly witches do not have bad hair days. Every once in a while, a strand may jump right at you. Their hairbrushes are laced with magic, and the hair caught in their brushes is then used in spell work. They always seem to have a lot of hair, too.

5. *Ageless*: Grandmother witches don't age like "normal" people. It is very difficult to tell their age, as if they have always existed in a time warp. I am sure they know how to tinker with time because I find myself warping it, too.

6. *The Color Purple*: Grandmotherly witchcraft is full of purple. Purple clothes, purple candles, purple crystals, purple plants, purple potions, etc. It is no surprise that purple is witchcraft's royal color. It has the highest vibration of all of the colors, so you will often see grandmother witches only writing in purple ink. My friend's grandmother, who is a witch, has a purple front door!
7. *Old Wive's Tales*: "Wait fifteen minutes after you eat before you go swimming." "Red sky at night, sailor's delight, red sky in morning, sailor's warning." Grandmotherly witchcraft is the origin of many old wives' tales, which often turn out to be true.
8. *Baby and Birthing Rituals*: Lightly tapping a silver coin on a baby's belly button, whispering a protection spell in the baby's ear, and walking the baby's house perimeter while singing are just a few of the grandmotherly witchcraft rituals I know about. The miracle of birth mirrors magic in so many ways, which is part of the reason midwives and witches have a connection. Grandmotherly witchcraft lore states that if a pregnant woman has heartburn, the baby will have a full head of hair. And the magic of being born "under a veil or caul" means that you have psychic powers.

9. *Psychic Powers Full of Predictive Abilities.* Witchy grandmothers can feel in their bones what the weather will be like the following day, they answer the phone before it rings, and almost always know the direction a relationship is headed. You will often hear grandmother witches saying, "it is as good as done!"
10. *Viscerally Connected to Nature:* The old witch living in the forest can tell you everything there is to know about celestial life. Plant and herb magic, the magic of berries, and long conversations with elves, gnomes, and fairies are just part of the everyday life of grandmotherly witches.

Ethnic Witchcraft

Black American witchcraft has its origins in West Africa, where Yoruba was born. Yoruba is a set of religious lore centered on recognition for ancestors and worship of orishas (a diverse group of deities). Those West African traditions came to America with slavery, and eventually combined with Catholicism, and other Western religions. By the 1800s, voodoo, hoodoo, and other fusions descended from West African religions. Most ethnic witches from this background practice with incense, water, and candles. Such minimal tools became a great source of power because the witches didn't have access to much more. Modern day African American witches have added a millennial touch to their Yoruba-based religions. Altars are erected to honor ancestors so they can ask their advice on everything from career advancement to relationships. Casting banishment spells with emoji magic to treat depressions, sage rituals, and crystal work are just a few of the modern black witchy ways.

Caribbean and Latin American Witchcraft cultures have vast spiritual and religious practices. Two of these are the foundation of Latin American witchcraft known today as healing magic (santiguos) and spiritual cleansing (despojos), which are the underlying powers beneath divination, amulets, spells, offerings, and concoctions (brebajes). Haitian Vodou, Brujeria, Umbanda, and Brazilian Candomblé are just of the few modern-day religions of Latin witchcraft. Constructing sacred altars and the use of white, red, and black magic to summon ancient spirits and demons, elements of nature for healing, love, beauty, and prosperity are some of the magical practices of the contemporary Latino Witch. Latino witchcraft practitioners have well known online services as sorcerers that can repair damages caused by jealousy, unfaithfulness, and humiliation. The amount of Latin and Caribbean witchcraft practices is higher in Canada and the U.S. than in other countries.

Asian Witchcraft is heavily influenced by Taoism and shamanistic divination. Chinese American witches can feel a certain disconnect from the resources available to them. Asian witchcraft doesn't really identify only with tarot decks, dedication altars, Aleister Crowley studies, and herbs and oils. Western occultism can offer Asian witches peace of mind, but they really would like to witness shamans telling fortunes on the street by face-reading. Mantic and magic arts are prominent in Chinese, Korean, and Japanese life. Buddhism and Daoism are important aspects of Asian popular beliefs and work as vehicles for transferring the magical lore of Asia, which is set in a framework of Chinese traditions. There are blurred boundaries between the occult sciences and the concepts of dualism (yin-yang), and of wuxing (earth, fire, metal, water, and wood), similar to the Wiccan connection to the elements. Belief in the magical powers of water, fire, air, earth, and spirit, as well as astrology, numerology, and other occult theoretically based religious beliefs is common among Asian witchcraft practices and other ancient religions. Symbols of the calendar not only mark the passage of time, but also make up the succession of celestials whose powers of magic can be invoked through talisman and spells.

Seidr/Norse Witch

Norse witchcraft is based mainly on medieval texts, such as the Eddas, documented after Christianization. These writings are made of beliefs and stories that were commonly held by Northern Germanic tribes. Norse, Scandinavian or Viking mythology laid the groundwork for the legends and beliefs of the people of Scandinavia, and Norse paganism.

Seidr

Seidr means witchcraft or sorcery in the old Norse language. It involves manipulative magic, called *galdrar*, and divination, usually practiced by women known as *Völva*. There were male *seidrs*, but they were generally held in less esteem. Goddesses of Norse mythology, such as Freya and others, were *seidr* magicians, as was Odin, who was harassed by Loki for practicing it, because it was considered to be unmanly. Freya was Odin's *siedr* teacher.

Völva

A *Völva* was known to be a shaman, priestess, or wise woman in Norse paganism. These priestesses were among the highly respected elites of society, who cared for the physical and spiritual needs of the people by methods of prophecy and herbalism. Some of the literature suggests that *Völva* were persecuted and marginalized during Christianization at the end of the Viking era, but they would carry on in the northern European notion of witch. They are recurring figures in Norse pagan mythology. A *Völva* practiced prophecy, shamanism, sorcery, and other types of indigenous magic. Mythological and historical portrayals of *Völvas* were thought to have such powers that even Odin, the God, consulted them for future telling. Early depictions of *Völvas* described them as old women dressed in white who conducted sacrificial rituals on war prisoners, and used sprinkles of their blood to prophesize about the future.

Georgian Witch

Georgia is a country of myths and legends that have been preserved as famous tales. Many of the Georgian folklore merged with biblical legends in the 5th century.

- *Legend of Tbilisi*: Today, Tbilisi is a lush forest where no one has lived since as early as 450 AD. Legend holds that King Vakhtang I Gorgasali of Iberia went into the woods hunting with a falcon by his side. The falcon hunted a pheasant, but in their struggle, both birds fell into the stream. When the King's army located the birds, they had been boiled, as the water was hot. The King was so impressed that he built a city in their honor. The capital of Georgia is Tpili, an old Georgian word meaning 'warm'.

- *"Fourth glass is of the devil:"* This is a legend about wine. When God was living on the earth, he wanted to make an easier life for those who were cast from heaven and sent to work hard on the earth. After contemplating for a long time, God decided that he would create a drink that would allow humans to take a short trip back to heaven. It was believed that God invited all of the angels, demons, and the devil to the first wine tasting. The wine was liked by everyone, including the devil, but as usual, the devil wanted to compete with God, so he created chacha (a potent alcoholic beverage) and asked God to taste it. After God drank four glasses of chacha, he said "those who drink less than four glasses of chacha will be on my side and those who drink four or more, they are on yours." When the Elders of Tianeti drink and feast, they refer to the fourth glass of wine as being "of the devil" and avoid drinking it.
- *St George of Mukhura and Devi (The Giant)*: St. George once lived upon the earth, and he went to the Mukhura village where many Devi (giants) lived. When he wanted to go on

a giant hunt, he told his deacon to leave the church doors closed unless the person sticks their little finger through the peephole. This would signal to St. George that he can attack a Devi. When it next happened, the deacon kept the door closed and St. George came running and defeated the giant with great strength. He threw the giant into a ravine and a lake magically appeared. Today, Devi Lake is a place where people go to throw stones into the lake and ask for rain.

Sun Witchcraft

Sun or solar magic can be used anytime, anywhere, by anyone, as long as there is sunshine. Sunrise to sunset and throughout the day, various times have their own strengths, which should be considered when casting spells. For instance, spells that are about new beginnings and fresh starts should be cast at sunrise and spells for power at noon, when the sun's power is at full strength. Sun potions, crystals, water, and any other magical objects or tools can be charged and cleansed by basking them in the sunlight.

There is not much of a difference between sun witches and moon witches. It just depends on the time of day that the witch feels drawn to the most or is most comfortable with. Some witches like to draw energy from the elements, like the sun or moon, and others from deities. The sun is usually thought to be a masculine energy, which is important to balancing the moon's feminine energy. Just like being a night owl or a morning person, it is a matter of preference. Not all sun witches are early birds. They can, however, choose the time of day or night to practice according to their intent. Sun witchcraft is outgoing and proactive, while moon witchcraft is much more reserved. Sun magic manifests as power, wealth, and physical energy.

Believe it or not, recognizing a sun witch is easier than you may think. They are more than likely out and about in the sun, getting a tan at high noon. However, remember to protect yourself from the sun if you're looking to tan when sun rays are very strong. They are the people who choose not to sit in the shade when they go to the park. You will often see them turning their faces towards the sunshine to feel its maximum effects. They prefer gold more than silver and enjoy warm colors, such as yellow and orange. Their energy is strongest during spring and summer and they are less active during fall and winter.

Moon Witchcraft

Lunar rituals have been practiced since ancient times and are still very much alive today. Ancient Babylon and Egypt worshipped the moon. Present day moon rituals offer you a sacred place for introspection, spreading love, setting intentions, and becoming empowered. The moon is a powerful source of self-love and self-care because it inspires you to question your goals, needs, and magical opportunities. The moon has eight phases; however, most ritual work involves the new moon and the full moon. The moon and the sun move into alignment during a new moon, balancing their feminine and masculine energy. The time corresponds with positive change.

When the moon is full, it is fully feminine and corresponds with intuition and nourishment. This is a time for magical creativity and personal growth. For me, lunar rituals are about listening to my higher-self and giving myself an occasional pat on the back. I cast my best banishing spells during a new moon and my best prosperity spells on a full moon. There really isn't a wrong time for moon rituals. All phases of the moon possess their own intention and meanings. Remember, the moon controls the tides, and two thirds of our bodies are water, so science also plays a part in your moon magic. Making moon blessed potions, and full-moon spiritual bathing are just a couple of ideas for making magic with the moon's help. Steps for moon magic:

1. Relax your mind. Full moon magic can take place five days before a full moon and five days after a full moon. Think of all of the unnecessary things in your life: habits, shame, biases, failed relationships, and guilt. Release these to the power of the moon.
2. When the moon is full, unplug all of your devices and put your phone away. Take all of your crystals and put them, along with several open containers (preferably made of clear glass) on top of your car or on a table outside. Place an empty bowl there too in case it rains.
3. With purple pen ink, write down the things that are creating clutter in your life. Then, burn the paper under the full moon with a white candle and set your intention into releasing them.
4. Use your fully charged items for your spell work. Use your moon blessed water for your plants, pets, and put a few drops in your tub or essential oil diffuser.

Star Witchcraft

The concept of star magic is as old as time. Medieval writings have intricate details about constellations, stars, and the best timing to pull their influence into your spell crafting, talismans, healing, and other forms of magic. The remnants of this ancient philosophy are recognized today in the form of birthstones. Most people take pause to stand rapt in awe when stargazing. Many of the deities we worship are star goddesses. Pagans and Wiccans take great interest in the stars for the plain fact that the pentagram, our religious symbol, is a star. Celebrating the Esbats goes beyond the twinkling point of the stars that hang like veils across the darkness of the sky. You can find your own celestial markers or learn those of the seasons. For me, as vast as the night sky is, it makes me feel oddly at home.

When you begin to work with star magic, try not to feel frustrated if you don't immediately know exactly what you are looking at in the sky. Start with one star, one constellation, and one season at a time. Learn everything you can about it and how to locate it again. Read as much as you can about start correspondences and classical mythology. Draw stellar energy into your spells and rituals and allow their energy to support you in worship, astrology, and everyday living. The simple act of laying on a blanket and staring up at the stars will connect you with your ancestors, as you will see the exact same thing that they saw. It will let you experience the echoes and wonders that have travelled the eons from the people of the far distant past. The stars' energies encapsulate the earth and embrace us in their stellar web. In the grand scheme of things, we are as tiny as a grain of sand, yet we are part of the wonderful and vast universe, and most incredibly, we can draw on the magic of the stars to enhance the quality of our lives.

Storm Witchcraft

The magic of storms is both terrifying and thrilling to harness. Connecting to the power source is the same as weather magic and elemental workings. Harnessing storm magic uses the storm's energy to manifest your intent. You can think of the storm's power as a type of battery. All of the air surrounding you is charged by the storm, including the ground under your feet. The storm holds in its great arms all of the classical elements: earth, wind, water, fire, and spirit. As a witch, you can learn how to connect with the storm and how to infuse your energy with its energy and channel the power of the storm into your spells. You can physically feel the massive energy of a storm coursing through your veins. It is so powerful, that once you learn how to work with it, you don't need any ritual or tools. But do carry an anti-lightning talisman.

Storm magic is untamed and wild, yet neutral. It holds negative and positive energies and can destroy and bless the earth. For this reason, storm magic demands respect. You can work with it, but you can't control it. If your ego ever butts in and you think you can master a storm, your magic will quickly falter, and the storm may strike at you! Hence, you should always have an even temper when approaching a storm. It can feed you energy and it can feed off of your energy. Once I tried to work with a storm after a very rough day at work. The storm lasted three days and left me in a blackout.

If you are new to storm magic, first try meditating during a storm. Sit inside your house with your windows open so you can feel and hear the vibrations of the rain and wind while thinking only of the storm. Pay attention to the living being that is the storm, and breathe its energy in and release it. You will know when the connection takes place, as an energy surge will radiate through you. For some, it is a shiver, for others it is a warmth. Once you are connected, call for a rise in the rain, wind, thunder, or request a lightning flash. Once something you have called for materializes, you are synced with the storm.

TYPE OF STORM	MAGICAL PROPERTIES
Regular Rainstorms	Love, friendships, healing, cleansing negative energies.
Heavy Windstorms	Addiction recovery, academics, breaking bad habits, sending messages to the dead, wishes, and mental spells.
Snowstorms	Transformational magic,

	purification, change, renewal, protections, and matters of the heart.
Fire Storms. A fire storm happens when the land turns ablaze due to the sun's searing heat getting brushed with the wind.	Power, courage, banishment, oath/commanding spells, and protection. *** USE CAUTION
Storms During an Eclipse.	These are extremely rare, yet powerful storms, which yield great magical powers. It is believed that an eclipse storm's energy can be harnessed to cure illnesses, banish unwanted spirits or energies, and achieve successful exorcisms.

Chapter Four:

Witchcraft Supplies, and the Witch's Common Tools

Usually, when people first learn about Paganism or Wicca, they run out and buy all sorts of magical tools. After all, the internet and other forms of media tell us to buy everything regardless of the need for it. Try to remember, before you hurry yourself over to Ye Shoppe for Witchy Doodads that magical tools actually have a purpose. Defining your brand of witchcraft takes first understanding that you are magic and that magic lives within you, in all of us, and in the universe. You have all of the tools necessary inside of you to become the type of witch you want to be. It simply means you are connected to the universe and the world in a way that means not harming them.

Sacred Spaces

For those who follow nature or earth-based religions, magic can happen in its truest sense when manifested in a sacred space. It is a space that is sacred because it is in between the physical plane and the spiritual plane. Be careful when choosing your sacred space. Think about the environment, lighting, and distractions, and use your intuition and creativity when designing your sacred space. Make it your sacred sanctuary. You can make it outdoors or you can make it where you can sit quietly in darkness to practice rituals. Alternately, make it where you can be in the sunshine and listen to the sounds of nature.

If you are going to create it in a spare bedroom or a corner in your basement, remove everything from the walls and give it a thorough cleaning, throwing out any clutter. Consider buying a new carpet and applying a fresh coat of paint; make it your own. Think about placing an altar there, with a chair for meditation, some candles, and maybe a few sigil pictures on the wall. Then thoroughly smudge the area. Perform a ritual of dedicating your sacred space to a deity of your liking.

> **Negative energy I toss you away**
> **In this space you cannot stay**
> **Negative energy I release thee**
> **My space is clean**

So mote it be

Altars and Shrines

Altars and shrines are magical places for spell work and rituals, and can be constructed anywhere you can find the space for them. While many witches and pagans place traditional tools on their shrines and altars, you can use whatever fits your needs and your budget. Just be sure you have everything you need for effective spell work and rituals prior to starting your ceremonies. An altar is not at all difficult to make. If you have a small table you can use, great! If you are going to do a lot of outdoor rituals, you can use a flat rock or an old tree stump. If you live in a smaller place, you can create your altar on a dresser top, a footlocker, or an old chest.

If you want to keep a private altar, you may want to make one that is portable and that you can put away when you are not using it. Find a nice bag or box to house your tools, and then simply get them out when needed. You can use the same bag as your altar cloth. You can also have altars which are permanent and sit out year-round, or seasonal altars you can change with the turns of the Wheel of the Year. I have two altars, one in my kitchen and one in my bedroom. Some of my friends have ancestral altars, with heirlooms, photos, and even urns of deceased family members or family pets. I still remember seeing my first nature altar, which was lovely. It had a piece of driftwood, two seashells, natural crystals, and other outdoor items that paid tribute to the elements and Mother Earth. Your altar is as unique as your spiritual path, so use it as a sanctuary that holds things close to your heart.

When setting up your altar, you will most likely want to include some magical things, but most of all, you'll want it to be functional. It needs to help you manifest your intentions. Here are the most common things that most traditional pagans and Wiccans include on their altars:

- Symbols of the four classical elements, which are aligned with the four cardinal directions. Use a small bowl of sand or dirt to correspond with earth, in the northern aspect of your altar; an incense cone corresponding with air in the eastern aspect of your altar; a piece of charcoal or a candle corresponding with fire in the southern aspect of your altar; and some blessed water in the western aspect of your altar.
- A Goddess and a God candle or candles representing the four cardinal directions. Also ready matches or a lighter for your rituals.

- Your wand or athame (dagger). You will need it for your rituals and spell work.
- Your BOS, Book of Shadows for your rituals and to keep track of your spell chants.
- Decorate your altar to celebrate a Sabbat or Esbat.

Magic Wands

Paintings from the Stone Age depict wand-type objects of power that are thought to have belonged to powerful leaders. In present day Britain, government officials carry what is known as the "wand of office" to symbolize their power. Witch's wands are used to direct and channel magical energies that are used to influence, rather than command. They correspond with both fire and air elements that are useful in rituals, spell crafting, and casting circles. The wand is considered to be a masculine apparatus, as does the athame, due to its phallic shape.

The wand works as an extension of the witch's powers, and due to its correspondence with the air element, it is associated with logic, communication, and intellect. They can actually be made from any material you feel attracted to. Mine is made of oak and it has a clear quartz ball on the tip, so I can use both ends when working a spell. I love my wand because it gives me a feeling of connectedness to my magic. I cleanse and charge it every day with a sage smudge and then I put it in between the leaves of my sage plant to charge overnight. It actually emanates an aroma from the plant that I can sense while I am working because I keep it on top of my keyboard for inspiration and technomancy. Historically, willow wands have been used for healing spells.

A lot of witches make their own magic wands (DIY projects) because they can use the materials they want to personalize, decorate, and design a wand to direct powers that they feel most connected to. Making your own magic wand allows you to bond with your tool and form a special relationship. A wand on its own isn't magical; it gets its magic from you and can act as one of your main tools for strengthening your intentions.

Athame

The athame is used in many pagan and Wiccan magical practices as tools for channeling energy. Oftentimes, it is used to cast a circle. You can use it in any situation when you would use a wand. It is a double-edged dagger and it can be hand-made or purchased at your local metaphysical shop. It is not used for actually cutting things physically. There are also numerous websites that offer guidebooks and instructions on how to handcraft an athame.

Athames are thought to symbolize fire, so using your athame to outline your casting circle is like writing it in fire. You also use it to call the powers of the elements into your circle and to scribe symbols in your candles and to write words on your candles or in dirt rituals.

Witch's Bell

For hundreds of years, witch's bells have been used to drive away evil spirits. The bell's ringing creates powerful vibrations which are the source of great magic. In my coven, we ring bells at Samhain (40 times) and at All Hallows (40 times). It creates harmony in a sacred space, can be rung to end or begin a ritual, and to evoke deities. Some witches shake sistrums, or use a ritual singing bowl or rattle. You can ping your bell with your athame, too!

The beautiful healing tone of a witch's bell can have various magical effects. They can banish negative energies and unwanted spirits, draw in positive energy, rid the air of stagnant energy, and attract desired energetic intentions. The bell is both a tool and a symbol for Wiccans everywhere. They also make a lovely sound effect for different types of rituals and can be used to guard your home. You can hang one by your front door.

Besom

The witch's broom or besom is used literally for sweeping a sacred space before a ritual. It not only cleans the sacred space physically but sweeps away negative energy and unwanted spirits that may have gathered since your last cleaning. It corresponds with the water element, so it acts as a purifier. Some of my witch friends have collections of handmade besoms, besoms from other countries, and besoms everywhere. They're like a coin collection. I like to drizzle cinnamon essential oil on mine during the winter months and tea tree oil in the fall. The magic formula for the traditional besom is a birch twig bundle, an ask staff, bound with willow wands (Wiccaliving.com, 2021).

Along with the growing admiration of handfasting ceremonies (an ancient Celtic ritual in which the hands are tied together to symbolize marriage), there is a growing interest among Wiccans and pagans in the concept of a "besom wedding." This is also known as ceremoniously jumping the broom. It originated during slavery times as a wedding custom in the American South.

Candles

Candles are a vehicle for transformational energy. When lit, the energy of a candle is transformed by flame and released. The magic consists in placing your intentions into that energy release and then channeling and shaping that energy to fit your desires and needs. Fire in any form is transformative. This is the same as in cooking or smudging. While fire is the driving force in candle magic, the color of the candle, the symbols you carve into it, and the shape of your candle are also significant. Given all of the correspondences, you can use candles according to the type of ritual or spell you are going to cast.

In both Western and Eastern societies, fire has been used to decode messages, interpret events, divine the future, and decipher prophecies. From ancient times to today, the bones of dead animals have been tossed into fires. When the bones crack from the heat, those cracks uncover the intentions of the Goddesses and Gods, guide the process of decision-making, and can tell your fortune. Indeed, for much of the cultural history of Western societies, fire has represented divinity, touted with anthropomorphic abilities, such as growing, breathing, feeding, devouring, and finally turning dead into ash.

Candles, in particular, are central to most modern witchcraft practice. This is because they are symbolic of all of the powers of the fire element and they can be procured easily and utilized in a controlled fashion. These all-purpose magical tools not only help to generate magic from intention, but they are also key to marking sacred space. Instead of emphasizing the destructive aspects of fire, candles symbolize its warmer, gentler, and comforting aspects and thus are commonly used in personal wish spells.

Witchcraft is about intention and transformation, your request, your desires, and your wishes manifested into reality. Candles are great communicators of our intentions; they act as bright messengers, carrying our intent into the universe where it can be felt. As the candle slowly burns, it whisks your intentions to the celestial realm. You can enhance your candle magic by adding herbs, infusing their magic with your candle magic to make your intentions clearer and more potent. You can also elevate your candle magic by carving various sigils onto your candle. This makes your intention visible during ritual work. You can also draw symbols on a piece of paper and place it under your candle during spell castings.

Candle Colors	Magical Properties/Day of the Week
Green	Fertility, nature, abundance, and money, *Wednesday.*

Red	Passion, courage, power, and vitality, *Sunday*.
Pink	Romance, compassion, friendship and innocence, *Tuesday*.
Yellow	Travel, success, imagination, creativity and happiness, *Sunday*.
Blue	Patience, truth, fidelity and communication, Monday, *Friday*.
Orange	Justice, creativity, ambition and joy, *Thursday*.
Purple	Spirituality, warding off evil eye, and wisdom, *Saturday*.
Silver	Dreams and intuition, *Monday*.
White	Peace, purity, balance and cleansing, *Monday*.
Black	Learning, grounding, banishment, and protection, *Saturday*.

Cauldron

The cauldron has been associated with witches and witchcraft for thousands of years. It is a womb-like, feminine vessel that corresponds with the water element. The Celts associated the cauldron with the Cerridwen mythology, which holds prophetic powers. Cerridwen is the keeper of the cauldron of inspiration and knowledge in the Underworld. There are various magical uses for your cauldron:

- Burn candles, incense, sage, or offerings
- Associate it with the deity of your tradition
- Grind herbs for magical purposes
- Fill it with moon blessed water
- Use it for scrying
- Use a separate cast iron cauldron for culinary purposes and season it well.

Salt

Salt has a rich history of warding off malevolent spirits, and newlyweds are traditionally sprinkled with it to ward off bad luck. Salt circles are also used for protection. Mix some burnt sage to make black salt for banishing spells and place some salted lemon water on your altar to cleanse your sacred home and purify your altar. Salt is a known witch detector, because they don't eat much salt, so if someone at your table complains that the food is too salty, chances are you are dining with a witch. Also, if you borrow salt from someone, don't give it back to them! Give them a cup of sugar instead. In some Pagan folklore, it is bad luck to let someone borrow salt, because they may use it to curse you.

Here's how you can use salt:

- Witch Bottle: Add salt to your witch's bottles for protection.
- Salt offerings to the Goddesses and Gods.
- House Cleansing Ritual
- Self-Dedication

Charging Daily Items

Charging and cleansing are two different activities. Cleansing removes unwanted or negative energy from your sacred spaces and from your objects. Charging is replacing that negative energy with energy that is beneficial to your intentions. When you surround yourself with only the energy your intentions will allow, your magic is amplified. At a very basic level, your magic is the ability to effect change in your environment. All things are composed of energy. This includes people, objects, animals, trees, buildings, and rocks, among others. In your witchcraft, you'll cross paths with many forms of energy as well: elemental, spirit guides, deities, your personal energy, the energy in your candles, crystals, plants, and essential oils, and the universe's energy itself. Some energies you bring into your environment are helpful, while others are not. For this reason, it is essential to familiarize yourself with the way varying types of energy make you feel so that you can surround yourself with energies that flow with your dreams, desires, goals, and wishes.

Charging

When you charge an item, you are filling it with a particular energy type. Charging can also be referred to as enchanting, empowering, or programming. You can charge a space or an item with whatever your intentions are. How you charge your magical tools depends on what your plans are for using them. Think of it as giving your tools their daily purpose. You can complement the object's own energy with the energy you add to it. For instance, a nail has the energy of being a nail (it's pointed, metallic, and creative), but you can charge it with the intent of making it a carving tool to scribe your candles or spells or to be more creative on one of your DIY projects.

Some items, like crystals, already have purpose, so when you charge your crystals or your candles you are specifying your intent for them. For example, rose quartz corresponds with friendship, so you can assign your rose quartz with a task of enhancing your friendships, building better communication within your family relationships, and so on. But take note that even though crystals, candles, and other magical items correspond with certain things, this doesn't mean you can't use them for other things. The energy innately belonging to an item only enhances and adds to your magic. Every and any item can be charged with intention. Usually, though, most witches charge those items they plan to use in a spell or ritual or items they are going to wear as a talisman or charm.

Items you can charge

Any object can be charged with your intention. Items commonly charged include:

- Crystals
- Herbs
- Cooking Ware
- Wand
- Soil
- Water
- Beauty Products

- Pens
- Needles
- Nails
- Sachets
- Witch's Bottles
- Candles
- Talismans
- Amulets
- Charms
- Seeds
- Essential Oils
- Jars
- Runes
- Cauldrons
- Seeds

For instance, you may wish to charge a green tourmaline crystal with a confident, happy, and lucky energy so that its vibrations will bring you prosperity. All you have to do is cup the gem in your hands to access its energy. If you are about to cast a certain spell, you may want to charge your candle for success; then when you decide to light it, it will be charged with your intent. You can add even more of a charge by anointing your candles or crystals with oil and herbs. The same holds true for any items you have charged with your intentions. If you are watering your herbs with moon blessed water, or carrying a sachet to bring you love, once charged with your intention, your items will hold their charge until it is needed.

How to Charge an Item

There are various methods for cleansing and charging your items with your intention. To begin, it is always best to cleanse your objects first by smudging with sage. Here are the steps for charging an object:

1. Choose an object. The object you choose depends on your plans for it. You may have a certain tool such as a wand or crystal. Maybe you just want to charge the coffee cup you use each morning, or the pens and pencils you use for your Book of Shadows. The list of items you can charge is endless.
2. Pick a charging method.
    a. I love to charge my items under a full moon and fill them up with lunar energy. The sun works too. The sun and moon charge and cleanse at the same time. Simply place your items under the moonlight. Full and new moons are the strongest. Focus your intent for a few moments and let them charge.

b. Charge with crystals. You can charge your crystals under the moon or various other methods and they will then be able to transfer that charge to other objects. All you have to do is have the crystal and the other items touch each other.

3. Visualizing: Rub your hands together until they feel warm and tingly. Close your eyes and rub them together one more time. Slowly move your hands apart, being careful not to fling them apart, or you'll have to start over. Feel the bubble of energy between your hands. It will feel bouncy and stretchy. Visualize the bubble, while you focus your intent into the item. You can slowly move your hands around the bubble to feel its energy. Speak or chant your intention aloud. Gently visualize pushing your intention into the bubble, and picture it changing color based on that intention (green for money, gold for abundance, silver for protection, pink for friendship, etc.). Now hold the bubble over your object and feel the energy moving from your fingers into the object. After a few moments, picture the item aglow with your intention. Note: Visualization is using all of your senses, not just seeing. Try to let yourself experience the vibration or

humming sound of the energy bubble. Maybe the temperature in your hands moves from warm to cool. Maybe your charge has a certain smell or taste. Practice getting to know how each item's charge feels during and after your work.

*Helpful hint*** It doesn't matter which method you use; charging is about the energy of your intention. Visualize the results you desire while you charge your magical ingredients and ritual tools. Holding your items and using tactile connections transfer your power and energy to them. Speaking your intentions aloud expresses your intent and makes your charge stronger. For example, you can say "I charge this pen through the power of the universe to bring creative energy into my life. As it is and should be."

Opening and Closing a Circle Ritual

Opening and closing a circle is a method for showing respect and thanking the elements for helping you to draw in their energy and release it. Face north and say out loud "Thank you for your energy, faithful earth; farewell." Next, face west, and release the water element by saying out loud "I bid you farewell, precious water, thank you for your energy." Next, face south, release fire, and say out loud "Thank you powerful fire; I bid you adieu."

End your circle ritual facing north and release the spirit element saying out loud "I am grateful to you, oh wonderful spirit; farewell as I close this circle and release the energy back to the ground."

Step-by-Step Instructions on How to Cast a Circle

1. Smudge your sacred space with sage, sweep it, and make sure it is clean.
2. Place a crystal or candle in each of the four directions. If you are drawing on the spirit element, draw a pentacle in which your candles and crystals mark the five points.
3. Face east and begin naming each element as you move clockwise to each point. "I call upon water, etc."
4. Enter into a trance until you are grounded and centered.
5. Form a connection with each of the elements, imagining how each one of them feels around your body: wind blowing, water swishing, etc., until you have named and connected with each of the elements.
6. Complete your circle facing north.
7. Imagine bright light shooting from the soles of your feet into the core of the earth, and then pull back its energy, and say out loud "Under the Spirit of the Goddess, with these

five elements, I cast protection within, above, and below this circle."
8. You are now ready for spell work.

Chapter Five:

Herbal Magic for Witches

My garden is a sacred and magical place, and you can make yours that way, too. There is a wealth of information on the internet and in bookstores devoted to garden magic. Many pagans and Wiccans have chosen earth-based spiritual journeys and often start their magical gardens at the start of spring. The very concept of experiencing the cycle of life, from seed to blossom to harvest, is the very definition of magic itself. There are goddess Gardens, lunar gardens, gardens devoted to healing magic, and many more. It is up to you what your garden will be devoted to!

Initially, there was no difference between medicine and magic. Today, we know that magic works on a spiritual aspect similarly to the way medicine works on the physical aspect. Without ancient European lore, science could never have developed successfully alongside medicine. There is overwhelming evidence supporting the essential role of magic in the origin of modern-day medicine. It's easy to underestimate the healing power of herbs. People have a tendency to go straight to over-the-counter medications for everything from headaches to indigestion. Western cultures, in particular, have been conditioned to take prescription medications and supplements to the point of physical and psychological dependence. The magic of herbs is that the only formula for their creation comes from nature itself. They are found in leaves, stems, flowers, and berries, instead of a prescription pad, and nurtured by the sun, the water, the earth, and everything that is natural in this world. There is nothing like the wonderful world of plant magic.

It is necessary to understand the differences between what magic is today and the role it played in medicine thousands of years ago. Historically, magic was built on the premise that the world was created by God and that all of life was connected in an ongoing chain. Correspondences between beings in one aspect of the chain and creatures or elements elsewhere on this continuous chain all are the purpose of God's creation. Life's *purpose* is the founding belief of magic. Since nature did not create anything by mistake or in vain, there must be a purpose for everything. The belief is that God left hints about correspondences, such as the flesh in a walnut shell resembling the human brain. Everything is connected. The role of the magician was to identify all of the corresponding associations and their exact magical properties, so they could be put to good use.

Similarly to the role played by magic in the history of science, herbal healing is as old as humanity itself. The relationship between humankind and the quest of healing naturally goes back thousands of years. It is noted in the recipes of ancient herbal remedies, historical documents, and monuments dedicated to preserving plants. Through the millennia of using medicinal herbs to fight against disease and illness, humans have continued to use bark, seeds, leaves, fruits, and other plant components as medicine. Modern day pharmacotherapy has acknowledged that medicinal ingredients are active in herbs and now includes them in a variety of medications of plant origin. Each herb has significant and special magical properties, stemming from its roots, petals, flowers, and leaves and can be used for cleansing and charging your magical tools, for healing magic, or for nourishment for your body and soul.

Essential Herbs

Cayenne pepper does a lot more than just spice up your chili, and nutmeg has a lot more properties that are underutilized when you're making a delicious eggnog. Your kitchen spices and herbs are filled with magical properties just waiting for you to add your intent. Not only will the following list of commonly used herbs and spices elevate the magic in your spells, but it will also help you to connect your magical side to your spiritual side and use them as a dynamic duo in your everyday life.

ALOE VERA

Aloe vera is actually part of the Lily family, and is related to garlic and onion. The Ancient Egyptians called Aloe Vera "the plant of immortality." The Mesopotamians used aloe vera to protect them from vampires, and to ward off evil spirits. This is also seen elsewhere with the use of garlic to protect people from vampires. The Hindus called aloe vera "the silent healer" and thought it to be a holy plant from the Garden of Eden. When I was a youngster and got burned or sunburned, I loved darting off to the backyard for some of that magical sticky gel that would make me feel better. It is a feminine plant corresponding with the moon.

Latin Name: Aloe vera, Aloe barbadensis

Folk Names: Burn plant, the desert lily, and elephant's gall.

Element: Water

Magical Uses: Healing, abundance, beauty, moon magic, protection, and love.

ALLSPICE

Allspice was used by the ancient Mayans as an embalming ingredient for their dead and also by the Arawak to cure meat. It makes a wonderful addition to chocolate, too. Allspice is named so because it highlights the aroma of many different spices, such as nutmeg, cinnamon, pepper, juniper berries, and cloves. It is a well-known remedy for toothaches, works great to freshen your breath, and helps with digestion. It has been used in healing spells for centuries.

Latin Name: P. dioica

Folk Names: Jamaican pepper, pimento

Element: Fire

Magical Uses: Increased energy, luck, determination, money, and mood enhancement.

ANGELICA

Angelica is commonly used by ethnic witches. It is medicinally used for heartburn, dementia, anxiety, fever, insomnia, arthritis, flatulence, nocturia, and a host of other ailments. Since ancient times, angelica has been a powerful healer and guardian of women. It is also kept in a white flannel pouch near a baby's crib to bring good health. It is also noted to cause sunburn when used topically on body parts exposed to sunlight, so wear some sunscreen if you are using angelica on your skin. Angelica is a truly divine herb used to communicate with archangels and the higher realms.

Latin Name: Angelicus

Folk Names: Holy ghost root, archangel root, wild celery

Element: Fire

Magical Uses: Protection, luck, breaking hexes, exorcism, prosperity, healing, and divination.

BASIL

Originally grown over 5,000 years ago in India, basil has become an important element in medicinal, culinary, and magical practices. The word basil comes from the Greek word for "king" and means "fragrant" in English. To the ancient Greeks, basil was associated with great wealth and royalty, hence its meaning. However, it corresponds with love and romance more than wealth and royalty. The association between basil and love is so meaningful that in the past, gentlemen tucked basil into their hats when planning on courting a woman. Next time you come across your love interest, offer a basil sprig to ensure a future relationship. Sprinkle some basil leaves over the heart of your lover and they will always remain faithful.

Latin Name: Ocimum sp.

Folk Names: Witches herb, king's herb

Element: Fire

Magical Uses: Astral projection, hedge riding, peace, love, protection, money, banishment, and purification.

CARAWAY

Caraway is a licorice-like tasting herb from the carrot family that has slight anesthetic characteristics that help soothe an upset stomach. It is an anti-flatulent (carminative), so it makes for a great after-dinner tea. The Ancient Germanic people sprinkled caraway in their tombs and coffins to ward off evil spirits. It is believed that putting some in your car glove compartment or in your wallet will ward off thieves. Folklore has it that when placed under a baby's crib, it keeps negative witchery away, and if mixed into animal feed, it keeps herds of animals, like sheep, together. It is masculine and corresponds with the planet Mercury.

Latin Name: Carum carvi

Folk Names: Meridian fennel and Persian cumin

Element: Air

Magical Uses: Love, protection, energy, memory, spiritual enhancement, money, healing, lust, and fidelity.

GINGER

Yule wouldn't be the same without my favorite magical spice, ginger! Used in gingerbread and ginger tea, this herb became a Christmas staple in the early 1700s. Ginger corresponds with Mars and the Sun. Make some gingerbread cookies, and the world will smile with you. Ginger is a warming, dry, pungent, yang herb used medicinally for illnesses triggered by damp, cold weather in Traditional Chinese Medicine (TCM). The famous gingerbread man was created by England's Queen Elizabeth I and quickly became a favorite Yuletide treat. In 1907, Canada Dry Ginger Ale was patented by a pharmacist from Canada and became very popular during Prohibition in the US.

Latin Name: Zingiber officinale

Folk Names: Ginger, African ginger, Cochin ginger, Jamaican ginger, and Race ginger

Element: Fire

Magical Uses: Grounding, love, creativity, the promise of new beginnings, health, dreams, and money.

CINNAMON

During the 1st Century A.D., cinnamon was a pricy spice used for culinary purposes. At that time, cinnamon was worth ten times its weight in silver. When using for magical purposes, make sure to use real cinnamon, not cassia. It is wonderful as an incense and flavoring for tea. When used in a witch's brew, it elevates your powers and increases clarity. Cinnamon and its warming sensation correspond, obviously, with Yule. I use it to charge and cleanse my besom, as it has antibacterial and antimicrobial properties. It is feminine gender and corresponds with Venus or Aphrodite.

Latin Name: Cinnamomum verum

Folk Names: Sweet wood, Ceylon cinnamon

Element: Fire

Magical Uses: Increases high spiritual vibrations, love spells, elevates psychic powers, lust, protection, healing, and money.

MINT

The magic of mint makes it a favorite among witches. It is very easy to grow, but keep it in its own pot or it will take over your garden. There are approximately 20 species of mint. The "Mentha" variety was originally found in the Mediterranean Region, while spearmint originated in Egypt and was taken to Europe during the Crusades. It was used as an "arm plant" by the ancient Romans because they would rub it under their armpits as a deodorant. It was also used by the Romans and Greeks in their sauces and holiday festivities. The mint's correspondences come from ancient folklore and have always been associated with deities. Mentha was a nymph who caught the attraction of Hades; soon they became lovers. When Hades chose Persephone over Mentha, she began to harass Persephone, who in turn beat Mentha into dust; afterward, Hades took the dust and transformed it into a plant, so that Mentha would live forever. It is feminine gender and corresponds with planet Mercury, and deities Pluto and Hecate.

Latin Name: Mentha piperita, Lamiaceae

Folk Names: Garden mint, peppermint, water mint

Element: Air

Magical Uses: Healing, love, protection, luck, attract good spirits, money, dreams, and banishing spells.

STAR ANISE

Star anise originated in Vietnam and Southern China. It has a rich history, dating back to hundreds of years before Christ. It takes 20 years to produce seeds and is a difficult tree to transplant. It was used in the early 1500s in Europe to flavor puddings, syrups, and jams, due to its sweetness. It is also used as a digestive aid in Asia. Shaped as an eight-point star, this spice corresponds with divine information, microcosm and macrocosm, expansion, and stability. Star anise is masculine and corresponds with planet Jupiter, associated with Sagittarius and Pisces in astrology.

Latin Name: Illicium verum

Folk Names: Eight Horns, Chinese five spice, Chinese anise, Illicium, Chinese star anise

Element: Air

Magical Uses: Hoodoo, mojo bags, good luck, anxiety, psychic awareness, anointing, purification, and cleansing.

How to Create Magic with Herbs

1. Making your herbs magical aligns their vibrations with your magical intention. Sometimes, you can accomplish this with the use of a single herb or multiple herbs in a blend. Their magic grows by exposure to each other.
2. The best way is to start a collection of herbs from either your own garden or the wild. The store should be your last resort for these herbs. Say loudly, "I am gathering these precious herbs for healing, love, prosperity, etc." Next, put them on your altar in a bowl along with corresponding crystals and candles, and start visualizing your desires.
3. Run your fingers gently through the blend of herbs while slowly and softly whispering your intention, for example "Petals of daisies, petals of rose, bless me with a heart that knows."
4. Now enchanted, your herb blend is ready for spell casting, or to be put into mojo jars to place around your sacred spaces. You can infuse rosemary, mint, lavender, and basil in

boiling water. Only use Pyrex for this, no metal. Keep a lid on the blend tightly so that no steam escapes. For every cup of boiling water, use one tablespoon of herbs, and strain before consuming. Also place some water in your bathtub, and charge your crystals and other magical items just by placing them next to the bowl.

Incense

Any combination of herbal materials mixed together with charcoal makes incense. Burning aromatic herbs and resins is a tradition shared by many cultures and has been for millennia. Not only does incense smell wonderful, but it is also used for purification, cleansing rituals, and healing ceremonies. For magical uses, the vibrational energy of incense is used in spell crafting accompanied by visualization, as well as background vibrations used in healing rituals. Grind your herbs with a pestle and mortar, and mix them with some charcoal in your cauldron, abalone shell, or incense burner. Cast away!

Frank's Incense Recipe

I grew and harvested this blend of lavender, rosemary, and lemongrass from my own herbal garden.

Ingredients

- 2 teaspoons of rosemary
- 1 ½ tablespoons of lemongrass
- 3 teaspoons of lavender
- 1 ½ tablespoon water

Steps

1. Using your pestle and mortar, grind your herbs into a fine powder.
2. Mix the herbal powders.
3. Slowly add five drops of water at a time, mashing the powders with a spoon's back, not stirring but mashing them together.
4. Form into a dough ball, just barely moist so it holds together.
5. Pinch a small piece of the dough and shape it into a cone, tall and thin.
6. Place it on a flat surface and let sit for two weeks.
7. When it's ready, just light the tip of the cone and enjoy (put on a fireproof surface).

Magical Powers of Trees

The Plant Kingdom awards us with many benefits, such as food, medicine, beauty, the ability to make paper, shelter, and shade. Specifically, the gifts provided by trees are incredible. Trees provide us with oxygen and take in carbon dioxide, providing the air that we breathe. They offer us food in the form of nuts, seeds, fruit, syrups, and berries. Some of my favorite tree foods include bananas, cherries, coconuts, pecans, and apples. Medicinally, the edible parts of trees provide us with antioxidants and anti-inflammatories, as well as other fantastic healing attributes. For example, for 300 million years, Ginkgo biloba fruits have been enhancing capillary circulation in people who use it to help delay the aging process.

Monkeys, birds, racoons, squirrels, and millions of other animals find a home in our trees. Trees are worshipped and respected in every culture and are surrounded by traditions of fertility and wisdom. We have all heard about the Tree of Life in the Garden of Eden. In the Old Testament, there are mentions of the healing properties of trees. The stealthy oak tree was worshipped by the ancient Druids; village elders would meet underneath it to absorb strength and wisdom. The trees' essence is divine and closely connected to humankind because they symbolize the cycle of life. Their seeds represent birth, and their falling leaves represent death, as they decay into compost. Just like our blood flows through our circulatory system, a tree's nutrients flow through its system, traveling from their roots, through their trunk, out to their branches, and back.

There is nothing quite like peak foliage. As the colors change throughout the year, it has an amazing visual effect that elevates our higher self. Suddenly catching the scent of an evergreen tree brings back memories of wonderful family times around the Christmas table. Just sitting in the shade is relaxing and can be a ritual in itself.

Here is a list of 39 trees and their magical properties:

1. Alder: Protection, resurrection, banishing, healing, and psychic intuition
2. Apple: Love, garden, healing, immortality, and goddess
3. Ash: Communication, healing, love spells, balance, knowledge, transition, fertility, and protection from drowning
4. Aspen: Endurance, peace, success, eloquence, rebirth, ancestry, and astral planes
5. Banyan: Divine connection, luck, protection, abundance, immortality, and longevity
6. Bamboo: Luck, protection, flexibility, fortune, and longevity
7. Beech: Creativity, second sight, ancestry, wisdom, and protection.

8. Birch: Creativity, fertility, healing, love, protection, goddess, inspiration, renewal, and birth.
9. Blackthorn: Strength, truth, protection, and authority
10. Bottlebrush: Energy, love, banishing, purification, and abundance
11. Camphor: Cleansing, exorcism, love, prophecy, dreams, healing, and lust
12. Cedar: Dreams, immortality, prosperity, purification, healing, wisdom, and longevity
13. Cypress: Healing, solace, longevity, protection, and grieving.
14. Driftwood: (This is not actually a tree, but it has been infused with the water and earth elements, so it takes on the magic of the sea, but still retains its powers from the earth.): intuition, dreams, grounding, moving, and ancestor work
15. Elder: Fairies, healing, protection, sleep, magic, blessings, creativity, and transition
16. Elm: Grounding, intuition, rebirth, healing, wisdom, compassion, and birth
17. Fig: Divination, fertility, love, luck, prosperity, and ancient ancestry
18. Fir: Protection, vitality, prosperity, birth, rebirth, and far-sightedness

19. Gorse: Fertility, protection, prosperity, and divination
20. Hawthorn: Cleansing, fertility, marriage, family, happiness, protection, wisdom, purification, and fairies
21. Hazel: Spirituality, luck, protection, passion, changes, and spirituality
22. Heather: Luck, protection, healing, changes, and spirituality
23. Hemlock: Shadow work, cleansing, and mysteries
24. Hickory: Transformation, flexibility, protection, abundance, kindness, and transformation
25. Holly: Death, healing, protection, courage, rebirth, and unity.
26. Juniper: Healing, protection, love, and cleansing
27. Magnolia: Dreams, clarity, love, protection, and truth
28. Maple: Communication, grounding, money, wisdom, love, and divination
29. Mimosa: Love, purification, happiness, and sensitivity
30. Oak: Fertility, prosperity, strength, success, luck, wisdom, ancestry, and health
31. Palm: Fertility, healing, protection, abundance, and potency

32. Pine: Emotions, luck, love, purification, protection, emotions, healing, immortality, and regeneration
33. Rowan: Expression, grounding, luck, protection, fertility, centering, strength, and writing
34. Sequoia: Eternity, wisdom, enlightenment, growth, and valor
35. Spruce: Enlightenment, versatility, healing, grounding, protection, and intuition
36. Willow: Motherhood, protection, wishes, healing, fertility, knowledge, relationships, intuition, relationships, and flexibility
37. Witch Hazel: Healing and protection
38. Yew: Strength, flexibility, rebirth, divination, ancestry, and death

Magical Power of Flowers

Flowers are manifestations of divine wisdom and beauty. Every flower has its own unique vibrational energy. Flowers are universal in their expression and they are readily available as a gift to us all. Flower magic means using a flower to focus our attention upon to manifest our positive desired change. The flowers that nature provides have been used in magic for centuries. Mother Earth is one of our connections to the universe and provides us with the ability to ground ourselves. Ritual adds structure, ceremony, and a certain excitement to everyday life, transforming the mundane into magic and the boring into the extraordinary.

Using Flowers on the Altar

At the center of our ritual and other magical practices is our altar. Using flowers to honor our magic is a beautiful way to focus and hold our intention. Placing those flowers on our altars illuminates our intentions. There is so much beauty in the presentation of a bouquet or collection of flowers that are specifically chosen for their energy and meaning they bring to any ritual. Their symbolism is an important part of how your desires manifest. Do not collect flowers at random when you wish to use them as part of a ritual. Collectively or individually they highlight the desire and intentions behind the ritual itself.

Flower	Magical Uses
African Daisy	Mystique, protection, fine-tuning energy fields, divinity, healing, and magical powers
Agapanthus	Authority, excellence, self-love, intelligence, intuition, confidence, self-mastery, and divinity
Alyssum	Comfort, peace, grounding, immunity, healing, staying true to yourself, and gentleness
Bird of Paradise	Self-awareness, recognizing invisible entities, insight, protection, sacred geometry, astral traveling, interconnectedness, and math
Bleeding Heart	Finding the beauty in pain, healing, love, emotions, depression, sexuality
Camellia	Alignment with the Goddess, confidence, authenticity, decision making, humility, prosperity, and receptivity
Carnation	Beauty, rebirth, love, healing a broken heart, longevity, and vigor
Chamomile	Breaking hexes, protecting children and animals, harmony, sleep, peace, prosperity, and soothing
Dahlia	Dreams, shadow talk, occult knowledge, and emotional transmutation
Daisy	Health, wealth, purification, and simplicity
Dandelion	Animal healing and protection, happiness, wishes, and divination
Echinacea	Health, service, fortification, support for

	those in the helping or healthcare industries, joy, and heartiness
Freesia	Clarity, transmutation, healing after birthing, depression, courage, and removal of blocked chakras
Heather	Ancestral connections and wisdom, luck, healing (physical and emotional), memory, protection, and transmutation
Impatiens	Divine timing alignment, grounding, and being present
Jasmine	Abundance, relaxations, attract love, joy, relaxation, and sexual energy
Kalanchoe	Grounding, protection, resilience, inner-strength, and harmony
Lavender	Clarity, joy, protection, balance, harmony, stress reduction, mend a broken heart, relaxation, healing relationships, and releasing shame and guilt
Magnolia	Ancient knowledge, Goddess energy, independence, personal growth, fidelity, wonderment, and awe
Narcissus (Daffodil)	Astral travel, mindfulness, romance, freedom from being stuck in the past, spirituality, and self-love
Orchid	Elegance, uniqueness, royalty, orgasm, fertility, wealth, love, beauty, harmony, intuition, and luxury
Poppy	Calmness, connection to deities, beating addictions, peaceful death, relaxation, sleep, release, and surrender
Rose	Abundance, love and romance, dreams,

	blessings, self-love, spirituality, protection, and secrecy
Sunflower	Happiness, vitality, potency, radiance, truth, strength, power, and sustenance
Tulip	Beauty, grounding, alignment with Goddess of love, simplicity, gratitude, heart health, and desire
Ylang Ylang	Joy, sex, peace, positivity, healing, and relaxation

Frank's Rose Petal Beauty Lotion

Roses are a midsummer classic and one of our most treasured scents. Romantic, gentle, and divine, roses are great for nourishing and hydrating our skin and are especially helpful for dry or mature skin. Make the most out of their beautiful abundance by designing your own fragrance skincare products, using organic ingredients to get that rose-smelling velvety feeling all over your body.

Designing a lotion is a bit tricky because you have to combine water and oil, which need an emulsifier. But it only takes three ingredients to make this hydrating rose scented lotion, perfect after an afternoon outdoors, after exercise, or before bed.

Ingredients

- Oil
- Beeswax
- Rose petals

1. Simmer 7 stems of rose petals in distilled water for thirty minutes.
2. Heat 50 ml coconut or shea butter oil with 5 g beeswax in the top of a double boiler.
3. Once your oil and beeswax are melted, pour 3 tablespoons, one tablespoon at a time, stirring constantly.
4. Put cold water on the bottom of your double broiler and stir continuously until the consistency changes.
5. Scoop into a jar and allow to fully cool before covering.
6. Cover and refrigerate.
7. Apply frequently and enjoy!

Charged Floral Water

Charge your floral water under the sun or moon, place it on a windowsill, or surround it with lit tea candles on your altar.

Flower Petal Ritual Bath

Spiritual bathing is a sacred activity. Sometimes, it's the only chance you have during a crazy day to unwind naturally. I have turned my bathroom into a spiritual sanctuary, surrounding the tub with flowers, crystals, candles, and incense. Bathing has been a sacred healing ritual in many cultures spanning the course of history. These sacred bathing rituals have grown since the ancient times when water has always been recognized as an elemental and powerful healing source. People in India, for example, travel thousands of miles to bathe in the sacred energy of water and seek healing.

In this spiritual bathing ritual, my hope for you is that you will find the inspiration to add a blessed healing aspect to your routine bathing. It is important for both you and your magic to spend some time showing yourself some love.

1. **Cleanse the bathroom**

Begin this ritual by cleaning and smudging your bathroom and all of your sacred ingredients. Did you know that smudging with sage or Palo Santo acts as an air purifier and reduces the amount of bacteria in the air by 90 percent? (Nautiyal et al., 2007).

2. Add beauty to your sacred space

After smudging, create a relaxing ambience by lighting a candle and adding some flowers to your bath so that they are in your line vision during the ritual. This provides a spiritual focal point, allowing you to dip into your meditative place. I sometimes just look at the flowers while I am bathing and intimately absorb their natural beauty and my connection to Mother Earth. Add some lavender or rose petals or petals of your flowers of choice to the water or add a muslin bag of dried flower petals to the bath for a floral infusion.

3. Connect to scent

Use a diffuser or other type of burning oil to elevate your senses. Again, rose oil or lavender are perfect for this step. While meditating, visualize the particles of scent traveling through your body and into your heart chakra. Picture a rose in your heart area slowly blooming with the aroma. You can also have some extra mojo by adding a tablespoon of pink Himalayan or Epsom salts. Salt water is naturally healing and a great way to detox your skin.

4. Place a Rose quartz crystal around the edges of your tub

You can also put some stones right into the bath water and visualize their healing energy nurturing, loving, and calming you.

5. Finish by Expressing Gratitude

Mindfully correspond with all of the sacred objects, enveloping yourself with the warmth of the water. Take the time to express your gratitude to each of them for supporting you.

Chapter Six:

Step by Step Guide to Rituals and Crafting Spells

While it is perfectly okay to use other spells, in fact there is a whole industry devoted to them, there are often times why you will want to craft your own spells. Sometimes, we just get that feeling of needing something personal and original. It is not as difficult as you may think because it is all about your intention.

Intention

Rituals and crafting spells have everything to do with intention. It's about making a decision about how you want your intention to manifest by casting a spell. It is essential to let the universe or deities know your exact intention. Remember, you are creating magic with other powers that be. Also, you don't want to mistakenly manifest the wrong intention.

The power of your spells comes from your thoughts and feelings. When put with your intention, you can harness the power you need to make magic happen.

Setting a strong and clear intention prior to beginning your spell is the best way to power it up. After all, it is the intention of the witch that makes or breaks the spell! Here is a simple formula for the beginner or intermediate witch to try:

1. **A specific desire (precisely) + the amount of time you want it to be revealed = your intention.**
    a. Using the word "I" and present tense verbs, write down your intention, as if it has already happened.
    b. Try it out with the following rituals:
2. Journal Ritual: Carve your intention into a candle and light it. While sitting in a sacred place with no distractions, start writing down what your life is like currently.
    a. Write down your intention
3. Ritual Meditation with Spiritual Correspondence
    a. Sit quietly in a calm state with your eyes closed.
    b. Decide with whom you are communicating:

      i. The Triple Goddess
      ii. The Great Horned God
      iii. The universe
      iv. The elements (air, fire, earth, water, spirit)
      v. Your intuition
      vi. Aloud, ask your higher power "What is my want?"
      vii. Now listen. Pay close attention to any sounds, sights, tastes, and smells. Your higher self will connect to your spirit guide.
4. Visualize Your Intention
    a. Meditate on how your life has changed as if it has already happened. Visualize the exact scenarios, and make any necessary adjustments.

Invocation of Hecate (The Goddess of Witchcraft)

Hecate is the goddess of magic and sorcery and of ghosts and the spirit world. Early in her reign, she was often invoked when childbirth occurred and for the rites of puberty. Often, she is the known protector of the vulnerable, including children, hunters, shepherds and herdsman, and warriors. However, she is not nurturing in ways of protection or motherly in any way. Instead, Goddess Hecate will bring vengeance to people who have harmed those she protects. In classical Greek times, sacrifices were offered in Hecate's honor, ranging from eggs and cakes to dog meat. She can be invoked to exact divine retribution against those who deserve punishment for their wrongdoings.

Wiccans and pagans, today, honor Hecate as a dark goddess, but that is due to her correspondence to the dark moon, the spirit world, ghosts, and magic. She is not easily invoked. November 30 is the date to honor Hecate. It is known as the Night of the Crossroads (Wigington, 2019). The following are ways you can honor Hecate in your own practices of magic:

1. Stroll down a dark road at nighttime, offering hymns and prayers to Hecate, and wait for her presence.
2. Dogs are most sacred to Hecate, so volunteer at an animal shelter or adopt a dog.
3. Tend to a neglected or deserted place that everyone else has abandoned.
4. Use torches in your rituals, not flashlights. In many art pieces depicting the Goddess of Witchcraft, Hecate is carrying a fire torch. It is a great way to intensify your magic and to welcome her spirit.
5. Dedicate your altar to Hecate.

6. Yew is known to be sacred to Hecate. Plant it on the boundaries of your property to invite her protection and favor. Be aware, however, that yew is toxic to animals and people.
7. Take Hecate to the point where two roads cross and become one. Burn a black candle there and call upon Hecate to choose the right path or to give a message to a loved one who has passed on.

Crystal Magic

Crystals are extremely powerful and surprisingly versatile magical tools. Modern magic practitioners use crystals for divination, healing, prosperity, aligning chakras, love, and much more. Each crystal has its own unique chemical composition and its own magical vibrational signature. Classified as inorganic matter, crystals are thought by witches to be alive because of their healing abilities for all living things. Electrical charges are visible to the naked eye when tourmaline crystals and others are hit with a hammer. This is clear evidence of their innate powers and energies. For witches, the powers of crystals are the same as those produced by nature or the elements. Since our thoughts and intentions are also energy forms, we can use crystals as magical channels to send healing powers and positive energies out into the universe. These energies then come back through the spiritual realm and bring positive vibrations and healing powers that manifest actual change in our lives along with them.

Connecting on a personal level with your gemstones is essential in working with them. Learning how to recognize and feel the vibrational energies of your crystals is how you initiate and strengthen your connection. As previously discussed, you can cleanse and charge your crystals with moonlight, sunlight, dirt, sage, water, and palo santo. If you do not feel the energy of your crystals by holding them in your hands, don't worry; eventually, practice will teach you how powerful they really are.

Here are some quick tips to "raise your vibes" and sense their energy:

1. Set aside predetermined notions.
2. Remove any gemstone jewelry (including any wedding and engagement rings). You will be able to palpate the vibrational energy of your crystal if there is no interference from other stones.
3. Unplug all distractions, such as smart devices, TV, radios, etc.
4. Pick a stone you feel an attraction to.
5. Your own vibrational frequencies will resonate with the crystal you feel attracted to.

6. Spend a few moments in a trance before picking up your crystal.
7. Practicing some deep breathing will help you to focus and visualize the crystal's energy with each deep breath. Imagine the glow around the crystal when you exhale.
8. Rub your hands together until they feel warm to align the energy centers in your palms with the stone.
9. Put the stone in the hand you feel is drawn to the stone or in your non-dominant hand.
10. Spend a few moments focusing on the energy of the crystal. While zeroing in on the stone, pay close attention to any physical sensations in your hands or anywhere else in your body (such as feet, arms, or head). Take note of any emotions you feel as well.
11. Pay attention to the temperature of your hands while holding your crystal. Can you feel any vibrations, trembling, or buzzing? Do you feel any tingling sensations, chills, or goosebumps? If you feel any of these sensations, or really any sensation at all, you are picking up the vibrational energy of the crystal.
12. As you inhale and exhale, imagine the crystal's energy taking form, allowing it to grow with each breath.

13. As you breathe in, take the crystal's healing energy into your body and through every cell of it.
14. As you exhale, gently share the energy with the Universe.
15. Without forcing anything, allow your gem to carry you on a serene journey where your body is encapsulated in its healing light.
16. Thank your crystal aloud.

Meditation

Meditation is a way to slip into silence and take a break from the noises of the outside world and inner turmoil, while tapping into the spiritual realm and total relaxation. There are many mental, spiritual, emotional, and physical benefits to meditation. It reduces your stress levels, relieves pain, and helps you to connect to your inner witch, improving your magical prowess. Meditation enhances your insight, giving you the know-how to communicate with gods and goddesses and the elements. Magical practitioners use mediation as a tool in preparation for rituals, divination, and spell crafting. The two main methods of meditation include concentrating on your breathing and a single mantra and mindfulness, which is aligning yourself with the universe and all that is sacred. It amounts to training your thought processes to acknowledge every sense, perception, and thought passing through your mind without getting stuck on a single one. Here is a step-by-step method for concentration meditation:

1. Sit or lay in a relaxed position with your eyes closed while wearing comfortable clothing.
2. Concentrate on inhaling and exhaling, feeling the sensations of each breath.
3. If you start to feel distracted, slowly restructure your thinking without self-judgment.
4. Recite prayers, sounds, words, or whispers, such as humming or affirmations.

Mindfulness

Mindfulness is a skill derived from the practice of being present, in the presence of the universe, in the current moment. It means getting the most out of each second that life has to offer, rather than consuming your mind with worries of the past or the future. Sometimes, letting go of what can go wrong, what has gone wrong, and how things could be if you should have, could have, or would have done things differently seems impossible. But it can be done.

Mindfulness is a survival mechanism, which allows people to be consciously aware of any approaching predators and prey. It makes use of all senses for gathering essentials. In the modern world, mindfulness can help us feel happy and centered in a world full of chaos. It gives us a way to manage intrusive, negative, and ruminating thoughts. In spite of our wishes, life happens, and mindfulness is the practice of training your mind to react in such a way that it will benefit your health and wellbeing the most.

Modern witchcraft has one simple premise. Your thoughts matter. Whether they are good thoughts or bad, whatever you focus your thoughts on will manifest in your life. This is also known as the Law of Attraction. We all know those people who seem to always have a storm cloud following them around. They seem to be addicted to chaos and conflicts. Well, the opposite of that is also true. People who think positively tend to attract other positive thinkers. They seem to be the lucky ones and are able to gracefully navigate through the difficult times in life.

Mindfulness is the grounding force behind modern witchcraft. Regardless of whether you're a magical tool collector, soloist, or minimalist, this part of the craft is often the most neglected. Worrying about things that happened twenty years ago or where you'll be tomorrow leaves out the living part of today. There are always going to be issues outside of what you can control, but accepting your experiences is a far cry from playing victim or being the VIP of your pity party. Feeling shame and guilt over things from the past is like carrying a 20lb weight on your shoulders everywhere you go.

When it comes to being a mindful witch, it boils down to staying present and controlling your thoughts. Try starting your day with a magical morning ritual. Set your intentions for the day, including when you will meditate, exercise, call upon the elements, and converse with your spirit guides.

Meditation is the key element to practicing mindfulness, so try the following ritual. On a full moon night, find a quiet and relaxing sacred space outside, hopefully in a natural setting, where the full moon is in your line of sight. If distractions interrupt your focus, imagine soaking the moon's energy through your mind's eye. Imagine the moonlight filling your body with a soothing brightness and mental clarity. Or try mindfully watching the sunrise, or focusing on the aroma and taste of your morning cup of coffee and bring yourself into a state of peacefulness.

The goal of meditation and mindfulness is not so much to control what happens to you physically, as it is to control your thoughts. When you do, you'll notice quite that this also seems to impact what happens to you in the long run. This is the heart of modern magic.

Final Thoughts

Remember that magic is a skill set, a tool, and a way of life, but using your common sense should also be a factor. You can cast 1,000 spells for getting a new job, but if you don't get out there and pound the pavement and send out your resumes, your chances of finding that job are greatly reduced. Everyday life has become digital and fast-paced which can separate you completely from the natural order of things and the spiritual realm. The aim of this book was to show you how to practice self-love in spirit, body, and mind by learning and then integrating the ancient practices and philosophies of paganism and Wicca, the oldest known religion in human existence.

Wicca and paganism are nature-based religions which hold a common belief in the union of spirit, nature, and being. Pagans and Wiccans come from every ethnicity, cultural background, socio-economic status, sexual orientation, gender, and walk of life. The pagan lifestyle, including Wicca, is a beautiful existence that promotes a relationship with the celestial realm, inner peace, and powerful ways to commune with the elements and all that is the universe.

We have talked about the history of trees, herbs, flowers, and plant magic to offer you a guide for your unique interpretation of natural magic or herbal magic. You should now be able to integrate them into your everyday life, while manifesting a spiritual environment to work and practice your craft. Plants and trees, coupled with crystals, candles, and essential oils are essential components of witchcraft. A charm, potion, spell, or ritual is only as good as the ingredients you incorporate into it. Many individuals use crystal and herbal magic for astral projection, increasing spiritual energy, aligning their chakras, giving offerings, and powering up their spells.

Spiritual energy is a life force that exists everywhere. It exists in the celestial realm, in empty spaces, within the smallest of molecules, and throughout galaxies. You can raise your spiritual energy by practicing mindfulness and owning a sense of inner peace. The union of peace, love, and joy is what empowers and strengthens your vibrational energies. It is important to keep in consideration that the static and noise surrounding us can interfere with our connections to the deities. Spirit guides are macrocosmic forces with a strong desire to help. Limiting the noise and the use of technology can help you to experience the fullness of life and open doors to wonderful opportunities, if you are able and willing to be present in the moment.

I hope that you enjoy this book as much as I loved writing it. If you do, it would be wonderful if you could take a short minute and leave a review on Amazon as soon as you can, as your kind feedback is much appreciated and so very important. Thank you.

Sources

Chevalier, G., Patel, S., Weiss L, Chopra D, & Mills PJ. (2019).The effects of grounding (Earthing) on bodyworkers' pain and overall quality of life: A randomized controlled trial. *Explore (NY)*15(3):181-190. doi: 10.1016/j.explore.2018.10.001. Epub 2018 Oct 11. PMID: 30448083.

Doyle, E. (2016). Wicca: History, belief, and community in modern Pagan Witchcraft. *Brighton, Chicago, and Toronto: Sussex Academic Press.* ISBN 978-1-84519-754-4.

Fra. A.o.C. (2002). *A short treatise on the history, culture and practices of The Hermetic Order of the Golden Dawn.* https://web.archive.org/web/20070928121719/http://www.osogd.org/library/biscuits/history.html

Grimassi, R. (2000). Encyclopedia of Wicca & Witchcraft. *Llewellyn Publications*. ISBN 1-56718-257-7, ISBN 978-1-56718-257-

Guiley, R. (2008). Church and School of Wicca". *The Encyclopedia of Witches, Witchcraft and Wicca* (third ed.). New York: Checkmark Books. pp. 61–62. ISBN 978-0816071043.

Nautiyal, C., Chauhan, P., & Nene,Y. (2007). Medicinal smoke can completely eliminate diverse plant and human pathogenic bacteria of the air within confined space. *J Ethnopharmacol.* 3;114(3):446-51. Epub 2007 Aug 28. PMID: 17913417

Llewellyn Encyclopedia. (2008). Golden Dawn. *Timeline*. https://www.llewellyn.com/encyclopedia/article/35

Oschman, J. L., Chevalier, G., & Brown, R. (2015). The effects of grounding (earthing) on inflammation, the immune response, wound healing, and prevention and treatment of chronic inflammatory and autoimmune diseases. *Journal of inflammation research, 8,* 83–96. https://doi.org/10.2147/JIR.S69656

Stardust, L. (2021). How to use technomancy as a protection spell for your phone. *Teen Vogue*.

https://www.teenvogue.com/story/how-to-use-technomancy

Wigington, P. (2019). Alexandrian Wicca. *Learn Religions*. learnreligions.com/alexandrian-wicca-2562902.

Wigington, P. (2020). American witchcraft laws. *Learn Religions*. learnreligions.com/american-witchcraft-laws-2562884.

© Copyright 2021 Frank Bawdoe

All rights reserved

www.ingramcontent.com/pod-product-compliance
Lightning Source LLC
Chambersburg PA
CBHW021440070526
44577CB00002B/223